MW01691181

Fun at Work

Building Authentic Teams

Todd & Marsha Davis

Copyright © 2021

All Rights Reserved

ISBN: 978-1-80128-050-1

Dedication

The ability to write this book and provide solutions for today's workplace has to be dedicated to all the companies, trainers, event planners, and people that we have had the pleasure of working with for the last 30 years. We have written this book for you, the supervisor or department manager, the small business owner, the non-profit committee leader, and all those who aspire to be respected communicators with their teams.

Here's to you and your quest for building a fun workplace for people to come and engage in teamwork on a daily basis. Remember to have fun away from work so you can have *fun at work*. As we always say and teach, people who come to work happy are usually the ones who leave happy too.

Todd & Marsha Davis

The Fun Coach

ParkandRecreate.com

FunCoachUSA.com

Acknowledgements

Everything we write comes from listening to others sharing their stories, hopes, and desires to enjoy the company of their co-workers, the time spent at their jobs, and more. Thank you to all the mentors, trainers, and leaders in our lives who have shared visions and foundations for fun at and away from work.

As facilitators, we teach people to hear and share ideas and input through consistent processes. Our teachings come from people like you and those you work with on a daily basis. We have worked with trainers, meeting planners, non-profit executives, and community members who seek a solution to communication and a better quality of life.

About the Authors

Todd and Marsha Davis are the Fun Coach team based in the heart of the recreation and tourism popular City of Scottsdale, Arizona. Todd has a seasoned career in recreation. His experiences are vast and diversified. As a college recruit for basketball in 1975, he was hired by the City of Scottsdale Parks and Recreation Department. Since then, he hasn't looked back from or beyond the recreation industry.

While getting a degree in recreation services from Arizona State University, Todd worked for the City of Scottsdale. By the time he graduated, he was a full-time sports coordinator and auxiliary firefighter. His passion and drive for fun and recreation permeated his lifestyle as he played basketball, softball, and volleyball and enjoyed other outdoor activities such as fishing and camping.

In 1982, Todd's creative spirit outgrew local government. He retired from community services and pursued a vision of corporate recreation programs. As most visionary entrepreneurs do, he struggled to achieve his goals, and by 1986 his vision of corporate games took off.

Marsha and Todd married in 1988, and together they created Corporate Games, Sports Tournaments, and Team Building Experiences. By 2000, they had offices in five cities hosting over 300 events a year.

Marsha has a passion for coaching, competing, and helping people have fun in life. At 34 years of age, she went back to college, played basketball, and received her degree.

Their passion turned to helping people have more fun at work. In 2002, they started Fun Coach USA with the goal of bringing fun back to people at and away from work. Since then, together, they have continued to facilitate and provide programs to meet the goal of team or connecting people together so that they can achieve more.

Besides developing TeamPlay, VolunTEAMism, and Fun Coach, Todd and Marsha are facilitators, speakers for national leadership programs, and adjunct college professors. Their intuitive nature, combined with the ability to motivate and inspire people through common-sense discovery-based solutions, has made them a successful Fun Coach team for everyone: businesses, associations, and non-profits.

Their mission is FUN! Developing a sense of Friendship (F) among team members helps relationship building. It works by building Unity (U) and meeting the Needs (N) of both the individual and the organization. It sounds like an easy subject, but it's not. FUN is a serious business. It restores the heart, renews the body, and helps walls come down so that we can succeed and move forward as diverse, unique, and happy people.

Preface

Out of 10 people at work, only three say they are engaged. Only three say they have a *balanced life*. If seven aren't engaged nor balanced, they probably aren't having fun at and away from work. As fun coaches, recreational programmers, and facilitative trainers for the past 30 years, we feel there are still too many people who lack awareness of the concept of *fun at work*. Even though many in the team building industry have been playing their part to make the work environment more efficient and friendly, there are still too many teams who are disengaged and frustrated.

This has been an increasing concern as it has made work unwelcoming, difficult, and isolated. We began to grow concerned about the work our fellow peers and we were doing as it didn't have enough impact. With our experience, we were able to see some real-life numbers and statistics, which distressed us further because a large number of jobs had an actively discouraging environment. Why are there still so many places in America that have such depressing environments even after all these years of hard work? Is it due to leadership or team members?

After years of providing team-building experiences, we had a revelation one day that set us about and toward writing the book. The real fun at work is the way you communicate as a team. You see, the reason why even in 2020, America has workplaces that aren't pleasant and friendly is simple. People don't communicate and solve problems efficiently. Our goal is to assist managers, supervisors, and leaders in being the ones who the team members respect. We thought if they were to become aware of the benefits of friendlier and positive workplaces, they would want to bring a change.

There are many obstacles in the way of an actively engaged work environment. If people were taught how to overcome these challenges, things would improve dramatically. Therefore, we have written this book to educate everyone about how important and useful incorporating fun at work can be so that it no longer has to be a taboo in the workplace. We will also reveal the methods that we use for team engaging and building. We believe in the FISH philosophy, which is something we use in our teachings. It is one of the many theories and concepts that will be discussed and expounded on in the book.

Furthermore, we will share the tips and tricks picked up on, throughout our experiences, in detail so that you can become a facilitator, just like us. Our goal is to teach you key strategies, from the art of introducing fun at work to building authentic teams that have lasting workplace friendships. Moreover, to improve your personal life balance in order to live a better life at work and become a leader who shares their knowledge with others and those in need.

By the end of this book, you can expect to have learned how to become an engaging supervisor, manager, or leader. If you follow the processes taught, you will become just that. Good luck in becoming one of the best leaders out there by bringing Fun To Work!

Contents

As the book was being written, the world became more virtual. The same principles taught can be used online with teams. If you need more help, contact Todd Davis. Be ready for your people when they come back for human interaction.

Chapter 1: Why We Need Fun at Work

Oxymoron: A phrase that combines two words that seem to be the opposite of each other. According to the Oxford dictionary, it appears that the phrase "*fun at work*" is nothing but an oxymoron.

When someone says, "Fun," you obviously do not think of work. In fact, it is probably the last thing that comes to mind. Instead, you think of doing something that is a hobby for you, attending a party, or traveling. If you're at a party and the unpleasant subject of your job comes up, you are more likely to complain about the job, the co-workers, and your manager than you are to praise them.

Social media is full of people repeatedly going over the fact that they dislike their job. There are platforms specially designated for you to complain about your job, your co-workers, and your clients. There are numerous statuses and posts where people rant about their job and the frustrating management. The anecdotes and stories that people have to tell are funny, and imagining what they go through is upsetting. Thanks to social media, people from all around the globe, from all industries, unify and come together as one as they discuss the injustices of their workplaces. Every day, there are thousands of stories and memes being exchanged, all of them revolving around an identical theme, "Work sucks."

You may not be the only one who believes that fun and work cannot go together. Managers and bosses are just as alarmed by this notion as you are. The idea that employees are possibly having fun is scary because the perception is that it will adversely affect the office decorum. Moreover, what truly terrifies them is that it will impact their productivity negatively. Yes, having fun at work affects productivity, but it is completely wrong to assume that it will negatively impact employee efficiency. Studies prove that having a relaxed and fun environment at work leads to a higher employee productivity rate[1]. The concept of a workplace having a fun environment isn't new, yet people continue to be surprised when it's mentioned. What we find disturbing is that people are either unaware of or continue to overlook the various benefits of having a good environment at work. Having a job where the co-workers and managers aren't restrictive but give room for positivity is an appealing thing and an opportunity that most people wouldn't want to miss out on. If the co-workers get along, the company benefits immensely.

The obvious explanation for this is that when people get along, they look forward to coming to work. This means fewer absences. Another matter to note is that happier employees are likely to perform well. People who are content with their jobs do their best to perform and bring in better results. Demotivated and discontented employees are more likely to do the opposite. Their work differs greatly in quantity and quality.

Nowadays, workplace satisfaction isn't limited to the figures an employee makes at the end of the month or the benefits or security their job provides them with. As we progress into the 21st century, we realize that a person's basic needs have evolved. Or maybe they were always the same, but they went unnoticed or were deliberately ignored. People care about their income, but their salary alone isn't a factor that can compel them to stick to their job or do their tasks to the best of their abilities. If they are satisfied with their job, they will automatically perform better and accomplish more. Job satisfaction can only be achieved in a positive and healthy environment.

In 1943, Maslow came up with a hierarchy of needs[2] through which he explained the concept of self-actualization. He explained that people have physiological needs, safety and security needs, and the need to belong. Once

---

[1] Choi Y, Jwon K, Kim W. (2020). Effects of Workplace Fun on Employee Behaviors: Focused on Generation Y in the Hospitality Industry. Retrieved fromhttps://scholarworks.umass.edu/cgi/viewcontent.cgi?article=1096&context=gradconf_hospitality

[2] McLeod S. (2020). Maslow's Hierarchy of Needs. Simply Psychology. Retrieved from https://www.simplypsychology.org/maslow.html

all these needs are met, a person requires their need for *esteem* to be fulfilled. If all their needs are met, they reach the top, which is *self-actualization*.

This provides people the ability to perform better. It boosts their thought process, increasing their creativity, spontaneity, and ability to solve problems. In short, self-actualization enables them to achieve their true potential and give their best. Over the years, many psychologists have conducted various researches that reveal the beneficial impact of creating a healthy and fun atmosphere at work. As a professional corporate team builder, we help companies and their employees to come together, communicate, and create a better workplace environment. Todd has been in the leisure and recreation industry since 1975 and has dedicated almost an entire lifetime to helping improve one's quality of life or QOL. He completed his degree in recreation and leisure services from Arizona State University in 1980. Since then, he has been working to promote it.

Our company, TeamPlay and Fun Coach USA, encourages teambuilding through specially designed activities. These activities engage and include everyone and allow participation for people of all ages, personalities, and interests to enjoy every experience. Marsha and I work together to promote having fun at work. We design work-life balance concepts and solutions to improve the quality of life at and away from work. Through corporate games and team competitions, we help co-workers improve productivity by having some fun time both at and away from work. Our favorite workshop, "Get a Life & Have More Fun!" enlightens people on the significance of fun and how to have fun in their personal lives.

In 2012, we developed an interest in teaching at college. In the present day, we teach recreation courses to college students. Thanks to this, we have firsthand experience with the new generation which is important as they are the new employees being hired at workplaces today. Being a college instructor has led us to know more about their feelings, their behavior, and what goes on in their minds. This opportunity has given us valuable insight into students and how to get them to open up and interact during class.

Making the younger and the older generations work together and put aside their differences is difficult to do in today's workplace. It should be a priority for engaging both generations. The generation gap has done nothing but created an aversion and a divide between the millennials and the boomers. We need to bridge the gap and get them connected as soon as possible.

We must admit, we thought teaching the younger generation would be a fun endeavor. But we were somewhat proven wrong. Getting college students to open up and develop an interest was probably one of the hardest challenges that we faced throughout our careers. We are proud to say that we were able to succeed through our Team Talk process. With our experience as teachers and fun coaches, we have been exposed to both age groups and their minds. This has greatly improved the way we handle diverse age groups and turn them into one united, functional team.

Over the years, we have learned that the secret to a successful company is its workforce. The way the employees do their jobs can make or break a company. People who perform well are an important part of the workforce and people who do not are a liability. What firms need to figure out is the contribution managers can make toward their employees' performance, whether good or bad. It is essential to hire competent people, but it is even more important to provide them with an environment that lets them work effectively and efficiently so that they can achieve their true potential and provide the enterprise with maximized outcomes.

We write this book to reveal what makes a better team at work and how you can achieve that. As a professional with experience spanning over thirty (30) years in corporate team building, the importance of a healthy and encouraging work environment and a united team cannot be emphasized enough. With this book, we intend to simplify and revolutionize the current reservations people have about having fun at work.

You spend a significant period of your adult life at work. This means a lot of your time is spent working. It's a shame that a considerable period of your adulthood amounts to doing something you dislike, surrounded by people who may frustrate you. A negative work environment contributes toward a dull, demotivated, and negative mind. Living every day regretting your job choice will only add to the negativity. This physical, intellectual, and emotional downward spiral is draining and will eventually take a toll on your mental health. An organization that cannot address and improve its frustrating environment isn't a place fit for quality engagement.

What Is Fun?

Do you know how people say it's the company you keep that matters? Well, it holds true even in a corporate setting. You don't look forward to attending a party that doesn't have people you like or connect with. So, it doesn't matter if your workplace throws parties to encourage co-workers to get along if they don't talk and get to know each other. Our belief from experiences is that your fun is as good as is your communication with your team. Simply put, your workplace's level of communication is the defining factor of whether or not your work environment is a fun place.

This applies to both employees and employers. If employees do not interact, they cannot progress further. If employers do not communicate well enough, they cannot help employees progress further. As a result, the company will remain in an unwavering stagnant state, full of disengaged employees and managers.

As an employer, you ought to communicate better with your team members. You need to allow them to have fun while they are working. This doesn't have to be a celebration or party (although that may also help). Fun simply means an environment where the employees feel relaxed around each other. It is the inclusion of each team member so that they feel valued and important to the company. Fun is the ability to uplift people's spirits and remind people of their value to their manager, their organization, and each other. It is human nature to want to interact with others. You just need to make sure you encourage an environment where interaction is possible, whether it's with you or with your co-workers.

This book will cover how you can encourage and motivate your employees to interact. If your staff is unhappy and you wish to rejuvenate the culture of your company, then this is the book for you. If you follow the instructions and tips that we will reveal throughout the book, you will be able to create a healthy environment for your employees. Incorporating fun at work is essential for many reasons. An improved environment will reflect well on the company. It has various advantages that will be discussed in this chapter.

What Is the Importance of Having Fun?

Once you have successfully created a positive and healthy work environment, you will notice certain changes in the organization. An employee spends at least one-third of their day at work. Their performance will drastically improve if the environment they are in improves. Having fun at work has a lot of positive results such as:

Enhanced Motivation

Lee Iacocca was an automobile executive, best known for his development of the Ford Mustang and Ford Pinto while he worked at Ford Motor Company. He went on to create his own company later that rose to success. He was a man who greatly encouraged staff. He said that good management is all about being able to keep your staff motivated. A friendlier staff means a higher level of motivation amongst staff members. This motivation can be for several things such as their motivation to bring in more clients, provide better service to the customers, and perform better at their jobs. This is great news for the company as it benefits them and also increases the motivation of their employees.

"Start with good people, lay out the rules, communicate with your employees, motivate them, and reward them. If you do all of these things efficiently, you can't miss." ***-Lee Iacocca***

A Friendlier Environment

People have become so immersed in technology that they neglect the physical presence of people around them. This makes them unfriendly and leads to a lack of coordination amongst employees. A survey revealed that before 2000, seven out of ten people had friends at their workplace. This dropped significantly in the following years as it was reported later that only one out of three people has friends at their workplace. Team building activities can help solve this problem.

A friendlier environment implies that everyone is happy for their co-worker's achievements and success. As a result, they try to take inspiration from their successful co-workers while also helping their less successful peers to succeed. All of this will contribute toward greater productivity and a high success ratio amongst the employees and for the company. A work environment that promotes friendships and is full of friendly people is attractive to all old, new, and potential employees.

Reduced Stress

Working together for eight or more hours in a tense environment can have a negative impact on even the best of employees. No matter how much their resume depicts that a person has *the ability to provide solutions under pressure*, it is only natural for them to give in eventually if they are constantly bombarded with pressure. On the other hand, a friendly environment ensures that there are very few factors that can contribute to tension amongst employees. This, in turn, reduces stress, thereby making employees perform better.

Increased Employee Loyalty & Lower Turnover Rate

High turnover rates are a source of inconsistency for lower productivity within a company resulting in a lack of unity. All of these mixed together is a recipe for dysfunction and a damaging culture for the business. Training new employees over and over again is a considerable waste of time and resources. Furthermore, a high turnover rate means a bad reputation for the company.

Talented above-average employees always consider the corporate culture before accepting a job offer. With a better work environment, you can make sure that your company is free from most problems associated with frustrated employees. A negative environment can upset the system of a well-structured organization, and so, all factors that can contribute toward negativity must be avoided at all costs. A lower turnover rate is always beneficial to your business. All of this will ensure employees' loyalty to the company. An employee who is loyal to your company will not only try their best but will also refrain from negative behaviors. A large chunk of your business depends on your employees. If they tarnish the image of the brand in any way, it may impact your reputation and cost you money and loss of clients.

"The way your employees feel is the way your customers will feel. And if your employees don't feel valued, neither will your customers." ***-Sybil F. Stershic***

An employee who is loyal to the company will be extra careful in depicting the company as the best option possible for the client. They will ensure that their service is up to the mark. They will do so not only for themselves but also for the reputation of the business. They will go the extra mile just to protect their company's image.

Higher Level of Engagement

Once an employee feels encouraged, they will exchange ideas and offer suggestions. We've been in this industry for a considerable period of time, and the reason why we have been successful is the ability to listen to people and their challenges at and away from work. After that, we try to address them to the best of our capabilities. The problem these days is that employees feel undervalued because their concerns are left unheard. The organization chart holds people from all age brackets. In a company where a twenty-year-old is working with a seventy-year-old, there is often dissatisfaction. The younger employee is often repressed by the older employee, although they may have something beneficial to offer. In this case, the senior employee feels useless if their ideas are overlooked or disregarded. Workplace generation gaps are another prevailing issue that we are now facing in the corporate environment. If the employer successfully makes both generations feel included and satisfied, there will be a higher level of engagement.

A higher level of engagement means an exchange of ideas. A free flow of communication between all age groups can contribute to a solution that will be useful and innovative. This will also be beneficial for the company as the co-workers will provide guidance and solutions to each other over topics related to the job and outside the job. A trusting and engaging environment can open up the possibilities of the business becoming bigger and better.

Lower Absenteeism

As a manager or employer, you're familiar with people not showing up for work. This means you are also familiar with the excuses employees provide for not coming to work. Sometimes they are genuine, but sometimes they are far-fetched and ridiculous. The reason why employees do not show up is that they aren't motivated to work. Their work doesn't inspire them to become better or achieve more. They feel restricted by their co-workers. They feel insignificant and judged as if everything they do is under microscopic observation, and whatever *good* they do goes unnoticed. They feel suffocated by the people they work with, and so they prefer taking a break every now and then.

With a better, reinforced workplace environment, it is guaranteed that the absenteeism rate will drop. As a result, people will look forward to coming to work and avoid taking unnecessary leaves. Humans are social beings. Once they start getting along with their co-workers, they are inclined to show up more often. So, there will be no more excuses for why your employees didn't show up to work both physically and emotionally.

Greater Productivity

Increased levels of motivation, brand loyalty, and engagement of ideas are great for an organization. Decreased levels of absenteeism, stressful conditions at work, and turnover rates are equally beneficial for a company. Your workplace shouldn't be a restrictive, toxic place because it can adversely affect the quality and quantity of your work. What all of this amounts to is a higher level of productivity. A progressive work environment is directly proportional to an employee's better performance. You can observe positive changes if or when the workplace environment improves.

Having fun at work creates a positive ripple effect in the pond. Even the smallest of ripples will help create another ripple. Every ripple will have a positive impact on improving the work environment. This, in turn, will contribute toward making a more successful business. A successful business will also motivate you as a manager or a CEO to show up at work. It won't just be because you are obligated to go to work. As a matter of fact, you will look forward to going to work to hear new ideas or different success stories. Whichever way you look at it, incorporating fun at work will be a win-win situation for the enterprise.

Ever since we began working in the corporate industry, we wanted to write about having more fun at work. Now that we have dealt with a variety of organizations and accumulated vast experience, we want to share our knowledge and processes with others. You see, unhealthy work cultures are a challenge that we have been battling against for the last thirty (30) years. Despite all that, this is an issue that obstinately continues to linger in our workplaces, singlehandedly affecting the employees' productivity and the way the business is run. With this book, we intend to address this issue in hopes of bringing about a change through a platform that has always intrigued us. We will share our workshop methodologies so that readers can implement the teachings and benefit from them.

A positive environment makes a positive and productive person. People should come to work happy and leave happy. Certain steps must be taken to ensure this. Living in a positive environment is essential for a person's growth and performance. We can't emphasize enough the fact that happiness and fun shouldn't just be limited to the workplace but also taken up at home and away from work. Don't worry! We will go over this ideology later and explain in detail why the key to a higher productivity level is a person who is content with their life at work and at home.

Through this book, we intend to discuss other philosophies that we have picked up or developed for training over the years, such as the Pike's Place Fish philosophy. You will discover the significance of teamwork, its benefits, and the activities designed to be introduced into the workplace for team building. Furthermore, the book will disclose important tips for managers regarding how they can train their employees to become great teams while motivating each other to become even better individuals. It is our sincere hope that one day America will have a better corporate culture along with a unified and productive workforce.

Chapter 2: Team Workouts

Impossible: Used to describe something that cannot occur, exist, or be done.

Synonyms include farfetched, inconceivable, teamwork, team building, etc.

These are the sentiments of many leaders with a team full of people who have several differences amongst themselves when the idea of creating a positive environment is suggested. It's alright, relax. This is a two-step process that can't be done without effort from your end as well as your employees' end.

It takes time to build a stressful work environment and will take time to break it down. There's no blame game. You are not the only reason why your business is the way it is and has so much lack of connection amongst the co-workers in your organization. Have you ever been able to clap with one hand? Well, this is just another one of those instances where it takes two hands to clap. You and your employees together, knowingly or unknowingly, have made this possible. There are many ways to bring positivity back into the business. We intend to share basic concepts that work. Before jumping onto how a positive work environment can be ensured, let's first determine whether or not your workplace has a disengaged staff and environment. Only then can we go on to fix it. It's not easy to find our way in today's work environment, but we have made it easier for you and put together a list of team health signs for you to review. They will help you recognize at which end of the spectrum your organization falls. If you feel they exist at your workplace, then we're sorry to inform you, but your workplace is exposed to serious disengagement. If you do not recognize this, then congratulations, your business rocks!

Disengaging Environment for Employees

A workplace that fails to consider the importance of its employees is bound to fail. This is obvious because there is no input from the employees, who are the ones dealing with customers, handling day-to-day tasks assigned to them, or executing important affairs. They are the ones who face the challenges and whose feedback should be taken into account. If their voice isn't considered important enough to be heard, then there is nothing that can help the business thrive in the long run. This is simply because we are creating a work environment that teaches employees to be mediocre. Luckily, our exercises help the workforce overcome this problem. We teach them how to win and become achievers.

Self-focused Leadership

Such leadership includes the C-suite of the company, but the biggest problem is when it comes from the managers. A good manager is understanding, humble, and friendly. Above all, these traits are their strength and not a weakness. Employees who are on friendlier terms with their managers tend to perform better because they feel valued and engaged by the manager. Whoever makes a united, capable team out of their employees is an efficient and *good* manager. If the manager is too busy thinking of themselves to be above all others and isn't spreading positivity, it is only a matter of time before other staff members pick up on it too.

Lack of Positive Communication

Look around you. Do you see anyone talking? Is there any improper communication or coordination between your employees? Do people prefer hiding behind computer screens and emails to having face-to-face contact? If the answer is no to all of these questions, we may have a red flag. Conversations that include post-meeting discussions or projection of what may be happening do not count. Everyone is simply too disconnected from each other. The situation is so bad that although they are all put together, everyone just feels isolated. If there is always drama such as dislike of others amongst co-workers all around you, then there is an apparent lack of positive communication at work.

Low Energy Level

It seems no one is willing to do the work. It is a place where doing your work is a hard task to do. If the day starts with "Why am I here?" or a meeting is constantly bombarded with "Hurry up and finish," then the energy at your workplace needs to be uplifted. There is an environment where people are unwilling to do their work. Any hint of extra work will cause either of two reactions: fight or flight. There will either be resistance or disappearance. The quality of work also drops in these situations as the work is done without putting a lot of effort or thought into it. "Busy"ness does not always equal good business.

Lack of Motivation and Enthusiasm

Unhealthy workplaces tend to drain competent employees out so much that they become disillusioned with their jobs. This makes them lose their initial enthusiasm and motivation with which they started the job. They are also a breeding ground for incompetent, non-engaged employees who discourage others from performing well too so that they do not look bad. In such places, the level of motivation or excitement tends to be fairly low. The productivity rate is relatively low. If you are a good employer, you should know that just hiring the staff won't contribute toward their productivity level as much as motivating them to do better will.

Higher Absenteeism and Turnover Rate

A common dysfunctional work culture trait is that there is a higher absence rate. People do not feel like showing up for work. They have no plausible explanation for it, and so they make silly excuses to avoid working.

It doesn't just end here. Absence is not limited to the physical sense. It can be the absence of mind, attention, or even emotions. Whichever way you look at it, it's problematic because when people aren't around, work productivity will obviously drop. Furthermore, a place that has nothing much to offer, except frustration, will only lead to a higher employee turnover rate, absenteeism, or emotional disconnect while being at the office.

Lack of Dissention

All meetings are comprised of everyone parroting each other and saying, "*Yes, ok, or whatever!*" There is no exchange of ideas or anything that can hint at *progress* during this meeting. Any thoughts, feelings, or reservations that one has are conversed after the meeting and outside the conference room. The whole purpose of a meeting is to talk and discuss ideas, something which is disregarded in such workplace meetings. People do not care about these meetings and dread being a part of them. And why should they? They are forced to sit together in a room with people they do not know, in a meeting where their voice is not valued. So even if an executive or a department head has a concern regarding something or they think of an idea to be impractical or irrational, they will stay quiet and choose not to voice their concern. This arises from the lack of communication, fear of losing the job, or fear of the *B-word*, which we will discuss in the next point. Whatever the cause is, it is dangerous for a business.

Fear of the *Boss*

The concept is simple. All employees are made to think that their boss is a phenomenon, a god, and the eighth wonder of the world. A boss doesn't have to be a CEO only. They can be a team leader or a manager too. A boss is anyone who can hold a worker accountable for what they have done at work. The most dreaded B-word is an entity far superior to all other members of the organization, someone to be scared of. The *boss* feeds this fear, basking in the glory of being able to intimidate or be in control of employees. They are unaware that they are the sole person responsible for the inevitable downfall of their company.

The problem is that most managers do not know how to engage the workers. They are completely unaware of how they can hold their staff members accountable. They put on a *brave* face in front of the staff. This, in turn, creates many problems. Most managers aren't prepared for what to expect from their team members. The entire team is deprived of communication, and so the manager is unaware of how beneficial and efficient a good team is.

No Clear Vision

All good business leaders can create a vision, communicate the vision, own their vision, and with determination, drive it to completion. The modern corporate world is always fluctuating and trying to keep pace with the changing business strategies and market needs. This means these visions have to be changed and the goals that were set have to be adjusted. When these visions keep changing, it becomes hard for managers to keep track of them, let alone implement the leadership vision. They are unable to communicate the new directions to their team members. In such work environments, there is a clear lack of direction. Pre-planning seems to be a value of the past. The workplace feels like a constant state of change and no clear direction. The workforce is completely unaware of what the new vision of the company is because of how frequently it changes. Their tasks seem meaningless because nothing makes sense. Neither the directors nor the employees can see a bigger picture or plan ahead. If your business does not have a clear vision, then it is inevitable that it will be unproductive and inefficient.

The problem with most businesses these days is that they are unable to engage their true strength and their most important resource, which is their workforce. Yes, we have said this before, but it is a fact that cannot be stressed enough. This causes entrepreneurs and business leaders to struggle constantly and leaves them wondering where they are going wrong. The good thing here is that you have realized and recognized the signs that can send your business up and down. All you need do now is to take the time for your workforce and divide them into teams for some healthy and creative fun. Now prioritize this task and do your best to eliminate this threat against your business. It can be a tricky procedure, but that's okay. It's where we come in to help. You can make it work if you're determined to make it happen.

It is our job to help organizations and people to break free from their stagnant culture. In the last four decades, we have come across all kinds of organizations with all kinds of people and learned many different techniques we have adopted or created over the years. We apply them to our workshops, and it certainly does help. These activities work wonders to help all such challenged organizations. The first one we'd like to tell you about is *Team Workouts*.

What Are Team Workouts and What Do They Do?

These are carefully planned activities designed to build up a team. Just as a body needs to work out to stay fit, similarly, a team needs a workout so that it stays compatible and functions well, like a well-oiled machine. These activities help the team members lower their walls and *let loose* effectively. Here all team members are given a fun and creative challenge that puts them together and allows them to communicate and engage with each other. They have a time limit that works as a controlling factor and a challenging goal to meet that can only be met through group work. When people are huddled together in an informal setting, with all these factors carefully set in place, they tend to interact and open up. They do not have the time to focus on negativity or worry about their differences. What they do have is the time, focus, and energy for teams to engage with their co-workers. These activities not only help build a team but also ensure that they stay engaged together.

A team workout, with its guided steps, will ensure that your employees get together and talk while solving problems. The friendly yet competitive conditions in which they are asked to interact help because they do not feel bound by the usual *stiff* workplace norms. Seeing everyone in a different light helps create friendships. It is all fun and game, a light-hearted competition, unlike the usual competitions at work that lead to serious work rivalry issues and unnecessary politics. These activities challenge the mind as well since they make people use their brains and common sense to figure out what to do.

There's another thing that we would like to point out. The way you do these team workouts and the frequency with which you practice them also matter greatly. Team workouts help, provided they follow consistency. We have perfected the best way to do this through the development of TeamPlay, a blend of competition and problem-solving. These workouts not only build the team but also help to maintain the value of the team - Together Everyone Achieves More. A team workout establishes healthy interaction through problem-solving, but it works only if that cooperative or friendly behavior that stemmed from it is maintained.

The idea behind TeamPlay is that every month there is at least one team meeting in which workouts are given to the team. It doesn't necessarily have to be a lengthy challenge. It can be as short as thirty minutes. All you have to do is make sure that the challenge you give them is interesting enough and the time you have allotted them is enough for them to complete it.

For example, if the workout is a problem-solving activity that's thirty minutes long, then divide the time into three sections equally. That makes it ten minutes to plan, ten minutes to perform, and ten minutes to process what they did. None of the staff feels left out, alienated, or inferior from the rest as no one is favored over another and all members are equally included. So TeamPlay is an exercise that follows a consistent schedule, allowing communication and cooperation among all staff members.

Since it is an activity that emphasizes verbal problem-solving, it is a source of healthy human interaction too. The staff becomes engaged and works on solving problems together, enabling them to sharpen their communication and problem-solving skills. This activity boosts productivity. It gets the employees' minds to sharpen up, gets their brain juice going, and elevates their moods. It prepares the employees to open up and makes them more accepting of the idea of a meeting. It prepares them for a work-based discussion and allows them to communicate.

After this workout, employees tend to be more expressive about their ideas or reservations on a new or proposed idea. It is a process that engages the entire workforce in a healthy discussion and everyone communicates freely and effectively. Everyone starts valuing meetings and looking forward to staff meetings so that they can give feedback or ideas, which boost productivity. Overall, it's the complete package of all the right advantages rolled into one. We have already discussed that the disengagement of employees is a costly habit practiced in frustration-inducing workplaces.

But did you know there are 20 million employees who are actively disengaged at their job?[3] This is approximately 18 percent of the American workforce. Actively disengaged employees are those people whose opinions are unheard and overlooked to such an extent that they feel they are *useless* to the organization. It is not even done intentionally. Sometimes, managers are so busy and have so much on their plate that they are unable to dedicate their attention to the entire team they lead. These busy managers are so busy checking things off their checklists and completing their tasks that they are unable to slow down for their subordinates to create a healthier, happier, and more productive work environment.

By not properly engaging the employee or making them feel unimportant, you create many problems in the workplace. These many drawbacks include a lack of input and valuable feedback from the employees, which can help improve the way things are currently conducted at work. Without their feedback, the managers and employees cannot properly assess whether their strategies and ideas are working or not. It also negatively impacts sales,

---

[3]Tolman Walker. (2020). Why Employee Engagement Has a Direct Impact on Your Business Bottom Line. Retrieved from http://tolmanandwiker.com/employee-engagement-direct-impact-business-bottom-line/

customer service, attendance, turnover ratio, and company culture. Therefore, it is of utmost importance that an organization should try to improve the situation by addressing this issue. Otherwise, it will lose a lot of valuable resources, time, and money (or their entire business).

Statistics reveal that there is an age classification in workplaces that affects engagement. In 2005, a survey[4] was conducted that revealed some shocking results. While 32% of the workforce felt that they were engaged in their jobs, there were 51% of employees who felt that they were not engaged. 17% of employees reported that they were actively disengaged. It can be seen through the survey that millennials are the least engaged of all age groups. This is a shocking contrast because 33% of baby boomers feel that they are engaged at work, whereas 42% of the Americans who are over the age of 70 and are still working feel the most engaged at work. This indicates how the younger generation is especially left out and does not feel included. This was back in 2005. Since then, numerous surveys have been carried out. Their results show very little changes in these statistics, with the numbers reaching a frustrating high. Our goal here is to address this high number of workforce population who feels disengaged and to help decrease these statistics. To do so, we must understand what causes people to be unengaged at work.

The generation gap is one of the biggest causes of these alarming numbers. The millennials are tech-savvy, smart, creative, and adaptable people who can take on a change. Older people and younger people have different varying customs and traditions. They both follow their own methods. This is a common source of conflict between them. Management that favors the more seasoned generation of employees is unable to comprehend the effect it will have on its younger staff, as they could easily get discouraged. The younger staff members are normally reluctant to open up, give information, or exchange ideas. They may feel unimportant, undervalued, or disengaged. They don't have experience with communication. They tend to disappear

---

[4] (2020). Lack of engagement in the workplace. Retrieved from https://appliedpsychologydegree.usc.edu/blog/lack-of-engagement-in-the-workplace/

behind the comfort of technology which, in turn, leads to being reserved. They tend to stay quiet and do not speak up.

Disengagement should be discouraged no matter what, as it is very costly for the organization. Team workouts have proven to be an effective way to battle disengagement and other problems that the employees face against each other. These team-building exercises are inclusive and unbiased and require input and teamwork from the entire workforce – all ranks and age groups included.

As a matter of fact, teamwork exercises function as excellent icebreakers. As the people go through the challenge and the hurdle together, they come up with solutions. They start putting the needs of the team above their own and learn to let go of their issues, reservations, and selfishness. This works well to bring people together and make them a team. It creates a friendlier environment amongst the workforce as everyone becomes more open and welcoming. Working together in an approachable atmosphere creates admiration and respect in the heart of the workers for their fellow co-workers. A simple activity is all it takes to bring back direction and order in your office.

Introducing little activities and team workouts at work is a small tactic, but it can take you a long way. Our programs have transformed many teams. In the end, it all pays off when we see the changed behaviors and attitudes from participants. Clients have thanked us for the work we have done and the changes in attitudes for the participants.

When your workplace has a fun and engaging environment, things automatically begin to look up for the business. Who even wants to work in a stressful environment? With the increasing awareness about the importance of mental health, it is only appropriate for people to expect better from their workplace. For this reason alone, jobs in a tense atmosphere, with negative people and practices and disengaged employees and managers, are largely avoided.

There are plenty of reasons why your workplace should be a fun place and why you cannot afford to lose out on employee engagement. The reasons already mentioned and explained do not begin to scratch the surface. They are all a recipe for disaster, and their consequences can be long-lasting.

As a good manager, you owe it to your employees and yourself to have an engaging environment that produces motivated and ready-to-perform employees. It doesn't matter if there are factors that you can't control. What you need to focus on is what you can improve. You have the power and authority. Make sure you put it to good use. Be there for your workers and create a comfortable, engaging work environment that allows them and essentially your business to thrive. Positive communication and a healthy flow of ideas never hurt anybody.

"Good managers know that people have 'good' sides and 'bad sides' and that the secret of management is in magnifying the former and toning down the latter." ***-Ha-Joon Chang***

Keys to a Team Workout

If you want to stay healthy, you have to work out. If your team needs to stay healthy and happy, it needs to work out. Team workouts are designed as problem-solving, creative, fun, and result-driven team testers. Workouts consist of activities that provide time for planning, playing, and processing. We teach that the process of *performance* requires discussing the planning process as equally as the playing or results of the game. Collaboration is an aggressive approach to a common goal or objective. Aggressive to the sense, there is a consistent process involved in the team's problem-solving. Team workouts are designed to connect people through communication, cooperation, and consensus to achieve a goal or objective against time or performance.

TeamPlay is the way we design the activities to incorporate all of the ingredients to make for a good experience. The process of how the team achieves the activity, whether good or not so good, is your focus. Getting the *I* in team or *individual* to contribute is the objective of the team workout.

The 3 I's

- **Individual** cooperative participation
- **Input** through the team talk process
- **Ideas** generated from healthy conversations

Roles & Goals

Some people are builders, some are the creative ones who come up with ideas, and some just like to do it. Roles and goals are the keys to a positive workout and should be established prior to the playing or performance time. Everyone should have a role in the end goal. That is the secret, and by the way, planning is part of a role. You can still be successful if only two people play while four support them, as long as it is part of the plan.

Message-Driven Workouts

Retrieving the message in the bottle is the key to all workouts. Workouts should be driven by an outcome of what you intend for the group to learn, achieve, or reinforce.

Are webinars worthless? This was a question asked by a professional associate. Their team-building budgets were cut, and the executive felt people didn't value the webinar time. We would phrase it that whatever you do, do it well through an engaging conversation. Everyone is busy, so slow them down through the conversation. Ask them questions and engage them. What did you like about the webinar? What may work for our team? What is your takeaway from the time spent?

Teamwork Values of a Workout

The 4 C's

Communication: Generating input and ideas while combining creative thinking and team talk is essential to the planning phase of every game. Every activity has a process toward success, which has a higher value than the result of the workout.

Cooperation: Teamwork and team values, aka Together Everyone Achieves More, are the time spent in the interactive planning and playing phase of the workout.

Consensus: Activities provide a set time to plan before playing. Within that time frame, the team must reach an agreement. We suggest having a designated leader for every workout who guides the input process to the consensus stage of performance.

Commitment: We have discussed and planned. Now it is time to commit to the challenge. Commitment comes through established roles to achieve the goals of the exercise.

The 3 P's

People precede Performance and Productivity. This isn't a tongue twister but an important rule. Engaging people in the workout by utilizing the process of team talk for planning and follow-up processing is your main objective.

Planning: The foundation of the team workout program is the time spent planning before playing. Planning allows for ideas, input, and the game plan being set for the playing part of the activity. Planning usually is a set time limit. To be effective, it should include the team talk process to get everyone's input.

Playing: Every activity has a set time limit to complete the project with time pressure representing the real world. Most exercises are set against a performance goal such as height versus competition, being the first done, highest, etc.

Process: This is the debrief time when you want the discussion of what worked, what didn't work, and what could or would we do differently next time? Even if they succeed, the discussion needs to be facilitated in such a way that they also evaluate the planning time, roles, and goals setting of the game.

Chapter 3: Team Talk

Waste of time: This is an idiom that is commonly used to describe something that took time and required effort but proved to be useless.

Synonyms include fool's errand, futile attempt, work meetings, etc.

Many years ago, we attended a week-long training on the art of facilitation. In order to succeed as a facilitator, we were taught that you must have a process to achieve goals and learning outcomes beyond one meeting. This chapter will reveal why Team Talk works as a process and the need for managers to have a process to facilitate and lead their teams consistently.

The whole idea of this book is to initiate methods that can effectively introduce fun at work. We have already discussed our go-to method for this in the previous chapter. Team Workouts are the most effective way to incorporate having fun at work. However, Team Workouts aren't carried out just like that. It is extremely important to create some sort of healthy communication first. After trying different methods for years, we have learned that the best way to make Team Workouts successful and accomplish your goals is to adopt Team Talk and have the team establish a form of communication. This is why we perfected Team Talk.

As college adjunct instructors (manager of students), we sometimes dread *class time* or we could say meetings for our purpose. This is for multiple reasons, but it's mostly because our students aren't responsive and do not communicate well. So as a teacher, we can become frustrated with our students' lack of response. We can also see this in another light. As a manager, one might be frustrated with the lack of engagement from employees.

This is pretty much the same everywhere. When we asked people what they disliked about their jobs, they almost always responded with *the meetings*. As a manager, this may come off as surprising, but it is also the reality. Why is that so? Why is it that meetings are almost always seen in a negative light? We can also look at it from a different perspective. The logical explanation for this is that the purpose of the meeting is not achieved. Communication is the crux of a meeting, and that is exactly what is lacking in meetings nowadays. People feel that there is no exchange of ideas or any important information being shared in the meeting. These meetings ignore the employees as well as their ideas and feedback. These discussions focus solely on the manager and their concerns.

The key to a successful meeting is communication. Seven out of ten people want better verbal communication. At the same time, seven out of ten people agree that meetings are useless and considered a waste of time. This makes sense because, as we say, meetings only work when there is a positive process for two-way communication.

If you probe deeper, you will find that it does get more serious than that. We find from our work that about seven out of ten people feel out of balance in life. They feel out of place and their life lacks the balance they want or desire. Who are these people? The meeting hosts or the meeting participants? Let's not be quick to point fingers at the manager or supervisor because it's not always the leader who is at fault. Coincidentally, seven out of ten people have revealed that they are out of time to communicate, discuss issues, break the ice, build work relationships, or be engaged with co-workers. These people include all members of a meeting and all hierarchies of an organization.

Meetings are an effective tool that helps employees and employers overcome the challenges a business may face through healthy conversations. If done the correct way, meetings boost the progress of a business. Unfortunately, meetings have become incapable of benefiting everyone in a business. In today's age, the trend is that meetings are unable to achieve their motive and purpose.

As someone who has helped organizations resolve and overcome similar problems over the last twenty (20) years, we believe that we can help you too with the perfect solution, which will help you and your employees to view meetings with the same importance that they deserve. We resort to Team

Talk on such occasions and have found them to be invigorating, and never once have they failed us. They work especially well for the teams that are already somewhat engaged because their problems aren't as serious or deep as other disengaged teams.

What Is Team Talk?

What Is a Team and Why Are Conversations Important?

A team is a group of people who come together as one and work to achieve a common goal. All members of a team are engaged, and therefore they are extremely productive. A team is a force to be reckoned with. It is essentially what makes or breaks a company. Incorporating fun and introducing team workouts at work are the fundamental steps that ensure an engaging work environment for all. Now that we have taken these basic steps, we need to progress further.

In the previous chapter, we discussed disengaging work environments and disengaged people. We discussed how there has been a rise in the number of employees going through these feelings, and to this day, that number keeps increasing. Disengagement contaminates a work environment, making it unfit for employers and employees alike. If employees say they are engaged at work, it usually means they are on their computers engaged with projects all day or people away from work. In a work environment, there are many types of teams that exist. On the surface, these appear to be normal, productive teams. It is only when you see their work and productivity and have discussions with them that you realize it is only the idea of them that exists. The reality is a stark contrast to that. There is a serious lack of communication and coordination amongst co-workers, which has a damaging effect on their work.

TEAM is a simple and really easy-to-remember timeless acronym, which explains how teams should function and highlights the importance of teamwork in an organization.

Together

Everyone

Achieves

More

Let's focus on this so that we can decipher what exactly this explanation of a TEAM means.

One way to look at meetings is to consider them as a get-together organized by managers for the employees. The foundation of a team is the emotion of *together.* It must not be taken lightly. This coming together of people, both physically and mentally, is the most challenging part of the meeting.

Which manager doesn't want their team to perform better? It is only human nature for a manager to expect and want more from all team members. The problem is the way the communication is carried out. Team Talk has proved to be an excellent way of communication between people. Not only does it work well for all employees (managers included) in business, but it also works wonders for a business. There is no distinction between teams. Team Talk is a wonder. There is nothing it can't work on because it works on all of them. From sports teams to a board of directors or non-profit volunteer teams, Team Talk works effectively on just about everyone.

Team Talk has been created to provide a consistent way of being together, so everyone's input toward the goal of achieving more genuinely fulfills the acronym of TEAM. This means the entire team is involved in communication. It's not just 50% involvement. With Team Talk, we guarantee you will have the majority, not the minority, engaged in the meetings, problem-solving, and teamwork.

Let's explore the effectiveness of TEAM by looking at what happens when a TEAM doesn't exist.

Not Together

People are not interested in spending time together anymore. Technology has helped people stay connected in one way yet disconnected in another. The outcome of this has been that the more people go online and start connecting with others on social media, the more people go offline in real life and start disconnecting from people around them. This has made them isolated from others and oblivious to their feelings. People prefer being isolated so that they can hide behind their latest, different-sized screens. These people are no longer interested in what is happening in their surroundings. These are the mediocre type of people who just get by. They are capable of much better performance, but they are held back by not being *together*.

Not Everyone

The rise in the use of technology has also led to a lack of trust amongst people. This has made people wary of each other. Gone are the days when everyone happily interacted with each other. Today, everyone has their walls built up. Being or coming *together* is a real struggle for them. Commitment issues have also arisen because of this. *Not everyone* can easily communicate or interact freely. This makes *everyone* think that they aren't a part of the group or team.

Not Achieving

Your workplace becomes a room full of average performers. It is only because nobody interacts with or cares about each other. The evidence is all in the communication struggles, mediocre performance, and low productivity. People aren't fully engaged. This serves as a stone in the path of their achievements.

The energy level has hit an all-time low because there is no real motivation to perform better. Financial gain is no longer considered a motivation for people to perform better and do more. People want to be appreciated and complimented, even if they tell you differently. They wish for their efforts and hard work to be recognized by people they know and care about.

What will happen if you go into a room full of strangers and announce you just got your degree, master's, professional certificate, or Ph.D. in some complicated field? People will feign interest, some will congratulate you, and others will be bored with your success. They don't know you so, why would they care about your accomplishments? What it all boils down to is that nobody cares about you and your accomplishment or achievement, and you feel the same way about them. So, being appreciated in a room full of co-workers who don't know you and whom you don't know will have the same effect or its lack thereof.

Not More

With all these things lacking, as expected, productivity takes a severe blow. Your team may as well be a group of strangers. There is a lower commitment from co-workers, little to no teamwork, and a low job satisfaction rate. All of this takes its toll on the business and its profit. Human capital also represents productivity or profit in some organizations. *Not more* could be defined as a lack of volunteers, committee, and board members, as well as donation and support.

Teamwork in an Organization

So, what exactly is the meaning of this word that we keep mentioning? Teamwork is the ability to come together and respect individual differences and personality traits, if any, so that the entire team can perform better and reach their goal or meet their target. Every individual cooperates by putting their individual skills and expertise to use and helping their team members with it. It is when an individual thinks beyond their own self and looks at the bigger picture, the team's success triumphs their own comfort. Do you know how they say two is better than one? Teamwork is the best exemplification of that. Teamwork can be best understood through the words of Andrew

Carnegie. He was a Scottish American who expanded the steel industry in America in the 19th century and went to become one of the richest Americans in history.

He said, "*Teamwork is the ability to work together toward a common vision. The ability to direct individual accomplishments toward organizational objectives. It is the fuel that allows common people to attain uncommon results.*"

There are a number of benefits of teamwork. These include:

Increased Creativity Level

With teamwork, there is an unrestricted flow and exchange of ideas. Different individuals suggest different solutions to a problem. Team members sit together and brainstorm ideas to find more effective solutions. They are content with their co-workers and their jobs. This makes them truly care about their company. Teamwork maximizes the chances of an employee learning something from a co-worker. Everyone becomes creative and helpful. They work together to perform better. Their enthusiasm is contagious, and soon everyone in the organization begins performing better.

Better Efficiency Level

Every individual has a different skillset. Every individual has a strength. When working together, every member of the team works on what they are best at and what they believe they can handle. Constructive criticism, tips, and guidance from co-workers help everyone to diversify their skillset and achieve more. Efficiency level hits the roof as everyone plays to their strengths.

Greater Productivity Level

In the previous chapters, we highlighted productivity and its benefits. Let us now discuss this in terms of an example. For example, your business is in customer service. With the entire team working and doing their best to provide flawless customer service to all customers, it is expected that the quality of service will increase. Teams will be able to meet the needs of their customers effectively. The quality and quantity of the work will automatically increase as a result of teamwork. Teamwork is the perfect way to boost your company culture. It's an easy way to satisfy and meet the needs of all members of the organization.

"Talent wins games, but teamwork and intelligence win championships." ***-Michael Jordon***

You can make as many teams as you want, but how exactly do you get them to perform as a team? After many long hours, nerve-wracking projects, and tough clients, we finally cracked the code. The secret to teamwork is the ability to engage the team in a meaningful conversation. Engagement is not only the backbone of a team, but it is also what can bring in teamwork. Team Talk creates and encourages engagement in all types of work environments.

Teaching college students has provided us firsthand experience of knowing that if you ask students a question, the chances of getting an answer are considerably low. Most of the time, students just stare at you. On a good day, an average is three out of twenty people who are willing to answer or talk voluntarily. This isn't only because the rest of the class lacks knowledge or confidence, but it's also because people are no longer interested in being part of the conversation. So how to make even the most unwilling people a part of the conversation? It's easy. You can do it simply by engaging them. Team Talk guarantees 100% engagement.

In the previous chapter, we discussed how the younger generation and the older generation are now working together, even after diverse communication styles have found themselves to be at odds with each other. The truth is, despite their exteriors, the millennials and the baby boomers, and all people, want the same thing to be a part of the team and for them to be engaged. With our experience, we concluded that fun at work is the ability to engage a team in a meaningful conversation. Team Talk is the best solution to engage all types of people, skills, and interests in a topic or task. The challenge is to create consistency in conversations so that all want to participate in the process. Team Talk is a process that engages people through guided input and listening. The key is to use a process and stick to it.

Team Talk

Mission

The mission of Team Talk is to engage people in conversations where their ideas and input are valued and appreciated. The host becomes the leader and guides using a consistent process that invites input based on designated talking points or a brainstorming session.

Team Talk Objectives

- Designate a table host to guide the conversation with participants' input toward desired outcomes. You can be the host if it is your meeting and you only have one group. If you have more than one table or group, teach and assign a host to each table.
- Table host listens without commenting after input is received from each person in an organized format, creating value for all responses.
- Provide teams with a consistent communication process for staff meetings, problem-solving, or goal-setting conversations.
- Create human interaction that balances quick and deliberate thinkers for full engagement.

What Is Team Talk?

Team talk is a process that allows people to share, communicate, and discuss their ideas without the thought of their ideas being discouraged, neglected, or frowned upon. Team Talk is facilitated by a host who initiates the conversation by asking questions and everyone else who responds to these questions. That's all a Team Talk consists of, and if used correctly, it helps build a team up. It encourages teamwork and allows engagement. All it requires is that it should be done frequently.

Team Talk is a guided discussion that improves participation. This makes the workforce efficient by providing a platform for new and seasoned team members to engage and have their input be heard and given a chance. The best part about the process is that the guide of this activity doesn't control the engagement. They merely facilitate it. Everyone's individuality is given a chance and their opinions are respected. With Team Talk, all thinkers and talkers are on the same page.

Team Talk Process

The process of Team Talk is simple. The following steps should be followed to utilize Team Talk effectively.

1. The designated host guides the conversation. The host can also participate in the conversation by acting as the last person to give their input. It is also possible to alternate between hosts if they are trained properly in the process.

2. Based on the topic and time allowed, the host asks for *short, medium,* or *in-depth* answers from each person. The host starts the conversation from either their left or right side. That is the direction the conversation resumes in.

3. The host repeats the question to each person to *refresh the topic* and provide a consistent communication process with no break. The host says, "Thank you" after each person is finished to close out and provides equal value to each person's input. If participating, the host is the last person to share, and then it is the group that responds, "Thank you."

4. Participants are allowed to *pass* a question if needed, and then the host will come back to them for their input or answer after all have shared their response.

5. People can share similar responses without reservations or feeling the need to be different unless it is a brainstorming session.

6. The hosts and participants in the groups are asked not to comment on another person's input during the process. So any given time during this activity, the host and the particular participant under the spotlight are the only ones allowed to speak. The only comment the host is to say to a participant after hearing them out is, "Thank you for your input."

7. Once the discussion is finished, the group may continue in conversations at the table as time allows (especially with multiple tables).

Concepts in Team Talk

Team Talk Input versus Brainstorming

Team Talk is a strategic input process that is different than brainstorming, where people throw out ideas without rules or guidelines. Team Talk is a specific, point-driven discussion. Each person is to share their input on the desired or discussed topic. The facilitator or host poses the question, and each person has the opportunity to provide the rest of the group with their thoughts and ideas based on the types of answers. Types of answers vary from short to medium to in-depth answers. The leader is considered a facilitator, not a controller. Their role is to initiate and guide a conversation and walk the participants through the process without commenting on their input. Team Talk allows *everyone* to be together and carry out discussions on the topics with 100% sharing and input.

Facilitators, Not Controllers

Team Talk teaches hosts, who can be anyone with good listening skills, how to facilitate and listen dynamically to the input of the participants. Controllers may tend to talk more or provide their opinion after each individual's input. Controlling personalities can adjust their style to be more engaging with groups by becoming a facilitator. It's hard to fault people with utilizing a controlled format for meetings to be "efficient with time" and get everyone back to work. The challenge is that most people want to get back to their tasks before they even get to the start of a meeting. A facilitator guides the conversation strategically and can participate in the discussion.

Talkers or Thinkers

In our experience, we have observed that participants usually fit into one of the two categories. They are either talkers or thinkers. Most of the time, talkers say things because no one else will. This doesn't allow thinkers to have a chance to share their input. Our Team Talk process provides *round-the-table* guided discussions, with a question for each person to answer and give their genuine input. When it is someone's turn to answer, they have two options: they either provide their input or pass until they are ready to share. Thinkers have a chance to "solidify" their response, and when it is their turn, they are ready to answer.

With a deliberate process, talkers have to decide what they will share. Their input can be managed according to the response time set by the table host and the facilitator. Todd is more of a *talker,* and Marsha is more of a *thinker.* We also need a process to assist our roles and goals in life. It works!

With Team Talk, there is no room left for "leader" bias, as the host can only respond with a *thank you.* Team Talk is an ideal solution for disengaged and, in many cases, overly busy work environments. It has served the purpose of an icebreaker better than most team-building exercises countless times in the past two decades. Their results have been better, more beneficial, and long-lasting. Adopt this strategy, and your team members will thank you for it. If your organization is suffering from a lack of engagement and has started reflecting on your employees' performance, it is time for you to text all your workers, "We need to talk." Then go ahead and have that Team Talk with them. Although the response to this message will be similar to what is usually expected in such situations, we guarantee that the outcome will be different. It will be more rewarding because of what you have learned.

One of our attendees in a leadership retreat for a national association went back to their group and implemented Team Talk. She shared, "*We had the best discussions about the lunch meeting presenter and talked less about sports and things not related to the topic at hand.*" A recent training with an executive team through Zoom resulted in the *best conversations* they have had in a long time. Remember that a *process* works when used consistently.

This is the power of positive engagement.

Chapter 4: Park and Recreate

Take a break: This phrase is used to describe taking a short break or some time off work, routine, or studies.

Synonyms include take it easy, stop briefly, unwind, chill… all of which are impossible at work.

As Todd expanded his recreation career, especially from 2000 on, he identified another common problem found in troubled workplaces — overworked staff. In busy workplaces, most employees barely have time for themselves. These places are a whirlwind of activity where no one gets the time to pause, even for a little bit. Workers in these places do not have the luxury of taking breaks and resting their minds.

For most employers, overworking or overburdening their staff isn't that easy to recognize or identify. Sometimes, people put the added pressure on themselves, even if it doesn't come from the employer. They fail to realize how big the issue is. Most employers or managers, especially task-driven ones, do not mind giving their staff members a full load of work. Oddly enough, even a majority of the workforce does not mind taking up extra tasks at work. A number of these people later feel guilty or miserable because of their crushing work burden, but some people do not even realize what they are doing to themselves. They are far too busy accepting new tasks and doing more to realize that they are taking themselves to the point of breaking and that they are the ones driving their minds to a stagnant state.

Ever heard of the term *dangling a carrot in front of a rabbit*? At workplaces, the carrot is a promotion dangled in front of employees. Employees are tempted to take up more workload in exchange for certain benefits or a promotion. While motivating workers to be more productive isn't a bad thing, making them so busy that they hardly have any time left for themselves sure is.

Sitting behind your desk and burying yourself in work can be unhealthy. You may think you're on your way to success by chaining yourself to your cubicle, but that's not true. You're making your way toward the path of ruining yourself. You are literally burying yourself in problems. You are making yourself susceptible to stress, fatigue, loneliness, and the biggest surprise of all – lower productivity and efficiency. What's that old saying? All work and no play makes Jack dull. By skipping lunch and not taking any breaks, you are overworking your mind and body. Humans are naturally not wired to do that. We need rest, which is why we need sleep. It's simple science. Without sleep, our minds and bodies stop functioning properly. Sleep deprivation can prevent the body from producing important hormones. It weakens the immune system. It can be the cause of many harmful diseases.

It can even cause a person to have hallucinations. Sleep deprivation can also lead to death. Just as sleep is imperative for us to rest ourselves to avoid all these problems, taking breaks at work is crucial for us to avoid other kinds of problems that can impact our health and lives, both physical and mental health.

Constantly arming yourself with an extra load of work is neither a wise idea nor a healthy one. Let's discuss the price one has to pay for such hard work without quality breaks.

The Trouble with Working Too Much

Fatigue and Stress

By overworking, you are leading yourself to mental and physical fatigue. This can have damaging effects on the quality of both your personal and professional lives. You are forcing your mind to overwork, obsessing over details. It may give great results in the beginning, but this is disastrous in the long term. You are wearing your body and mind out, which makes life stressful for you and your team.

Loneliness

You skip all your breaks. You work yourself so hard that you have no time for any sort of break. Even when you are away from work, you are obsessing and worrying about your workload and tasks. Wrapping yourself around paperwork and hiding behind the desk lead you toward the path of isolation. As you take on more work, you feel more and more disconnected, which isn't healthy because our nature is designed to be social. People have a natural tendency to blend in with others, to be accepted, and to belong. Since you hardly make time for yourself, the chances of you making time for others are slim to none, which means the odds of you feeling lonely are very high.

Unusual Sensitivity

Being tired, overworked, and lonely is a perfect recipe for disaster. This combination has several problems. You begin to expect more from your workplace. You expect more from the people you work with. You feel like you deserve more credit and recognition for your hard work. You barely know the people you work with, yet you start expecting things from them. These people do not know you, and as we discussed in the previous chapter, your accomplishments are of no worth to these people.

This means your co-workers and team members *fail* your high expectations. This leads to disillusionment and unusual sensitivity. You become sensitive to every little thing. The smallest of things put you off. You get snappy, emotional, or frequently shut down. This leads to arguments, conflicts, or a lack of healthy discussions. This results in people becoming more *isolated* than *conversational* to the point that we bottle up our stress. This isn't healthy. All of it takes a toll on mental health, productivity, and the work environment.

Lack of Creativity

In the middle of this whole dilemma, it is your creativity that takes a hit. You and your original ideas no longer exist. Your mind is so exhausted that it stops working properly. The flow of new ideas and helpful suggestions stops from your end. Your mind is drained, and this causes your creativity to disintegrate little by little. You are neither interested in sharing your ideas nor are you interested in hearing new ideas from your team members. Their ideas do not inspire you. They feel like a burden to you instead, making it hard for you to make it through the day. This leads to mediocrity. Skipping breaks is like a slow stress cooker. It hurts everyone slowly but surely.

More Mistakes

As exhaustion takes over and replaces creativity, your work suffers too. Despite the fact that you work so hard on trying to focus, the brain loses concentration. You no longer focus on things and your mind stops paying attention to details. It isn't as sharp as it used to be. The mind has been worked so hard and for so long that it becomes *dull*. You lose focus, attention, and concentration. The quality of your work deteriorates, making your work performance *average*, as your mind becomes prone to making mistakes. The worst thing about this is that you brought it upon yourself.

Workplace Burnout

There's a limit to how long you can overwork and take the stress. After a while, it affects your thinking. Being stressed for a prolonged time results in a state of burnout, which is a physically, emotionally, and mentally damaging state to be in. It consumes you so much that you are unable to think, work, or even function properly. It negatively affects your personal life as much as it damages your professional life because the same burnout affects the team when these burnouts occur within them.

No Time to Bond with Other Employees

Without breaks, the chance of interacting with co-workers becomes limited. You do nothing fun with your employees or fellow workers. You become labeled as the *stiff one*. People begin to think that you are arrogant and think of yourself as someone superior or above the others. All your co-workers and team members are intimidated by you. This creates a barrier between you and the others. Nobody will consider the fact that you have a lot on your plate. There is no proper engagement from both ends. We have already gone over the many advantages of engagement and disadvantages of disengagement at work, but to put it simply, disengagement can hurt businesses because it lowers the productivity rate significantly. Be friendly to those you work with. You don't have to be their best friend or spend all your time with them. However, being friendly creates a healthy and positive environment that gives back uncountable benefits.

Decrease in Productivity

With all these unfavorable factors and situations created only because you didn't stop to take a break, your productivity level decreases. The one thing that you wanted to do inevitably becomes the thing you cannot do. Overworking makes you worry about the work too much. You put extra hours, energy, and effort into your work. All of it amounts to nothing because your mind is too worn out and strained to function properly. This lack of productivity can go home with you and impact your personal projects, and you feel even more stressed.

All of these problems stem from a small issue. It is shocking how one simple break holds power to affect so much. As a manager, your workload is more than the workload of your employees. In fact, as a manager, you are also a role model. For that, you strive to be the perfect employee by taking on more and more work and cutting out on your breaks as often as possible.

At the very beginning of my career, I, Todd, noticed the trouble that comes along with these little things, and so I vowed to make a change. For that reason, we perfected another method that I call *park and recreate*. This means to stop for fun. This method works for both individuals and teams.

"My back is killing me."

"Oh no, not that client again!"

"This has to be the hardest task I've ever been given."

"I was up all night, working on this presentation."

"I stayed late this whole week because we have our deadline coming in."

"I will have to delay my travel plans; work has come up."

"I promised to visit my best friend next week, so I will work overtime this week. That way, I can complete my work and enjoy the weekend getaway."

"I am so fed up with my work."

How familiar do all of these thoughts sound to you? For all the reasons mentioned above, this is exactly why you need to take a break. Park! Just stop everything you're doing. Take a deep breath. Relax. Take a break to unwind. If you don't stop for the little things in life, your life won't mean much. It's simple, really. You put yourself at risk in all these situations yourself. You leave for work unhappy. You go home unhappy. You come back to work unhappy. All of this is a chain of excuses but can easily be broken.

Todd was speaking to a small business owner who wanted to take their team out for a day of play. They were surprised to learn that half their workforce wasn't interested in spending time with co-workers, even if it was just for fun. They preferred going home instead. With the competition, disengagement, and alienation present in the workforce today, this came as no surprise. In fact, if we take a survey right this moment, the number of people who choose to go home will be higher than fifty percent.

This hasn't always been the case, though. Previously, teams were positive and united together, and people considered their coworkers as family. Let's look back in memory lane when it comes to corporate fun. Maybe then we will be able to see when and why the switch from positive work teams to disconnected teams occurred.

Todd was hired as a sports coordinator for the City of Scottsdale in 1977. It was there he discovered that games were used to unite and celebrate the workforce. Soon, he became experienced in organizing and managing different games for team building, such as softball, volleyball, and basketball programs. About 60% of these teams consisted of co-workers who had part of their day planned out for recreational activities.

So roughly, about 60% of the people coming in were co-workers who understood the value of recreational time. It was great to observe the friendships many of the co-workers had developed. Different teams of multiple companies came together to enjoy their time with their co-workers (who were also their friends) and grabbed a refreshment with them after the game. Those were the days of having, making, and taking time for interests with other people from work. Things were simpler, more fun-filled back then. Even corporate recreation was such a strong value that companies that promoted it instantly earned the respect of people and became an attractive choice for people to consider when applying for a job.

As a visionary of recreation, Todd left the City in 1982 to form Corporate Games, a small, privately owned business that focused on these values. The business became an outlet for the workplaces to reinforce team spirit and promote corporate recreation. He organized and held many successful team superstar picnics and sports tournaments ranging from softball to soccer and bowling tournaments.

The business provided organizations with the complete *Company Olympics* experience and became a pioneer of the Fun Olympics in corporate settings by introducing a personally designed obstacle course, including games such as quad volleyball and relays. Teams of all sorts and sports of all kinds were considered and included. All these became the key to a fun time together for all employees of businesses and companies, whether small or large.

The business prospered even more when Todd and Marsha were married in 1988. Their work expanded throughout the years, introducing and perfecting different new ways to incorporate fun for corporate groups and meetings. Together using their skills of programming and planning, this allowed their creativity and imagination to plan new ways to offer adult-friendly experiences for employees of a workplace.

Nowadays, co-workers are unwilling to walk you out of the building, but in the '70s and all the way to the '90s, things were very different. Employees would go to different states or cities for a fun time with their co-workers. In those times, even employee club bus trips to Vegas were popular options for co-workers to travel, hang out, relax, and recreate. That is the power of friendships and common interests.

Even simple things such as bus rides become important and valued when done together with other co-workers. Playing sports has united people for centuries, so people unite to play sports or give time to shared hobbies and interests. They take their recreational time seriously. This boosts the work morale and positively influences the productivity of a business.

- 1988, our business discovered that the *real money* was in the *meeting industry*, and so we began to focus on that target market. By 2000, we were able to host over three hundred clients and events per year.

- In the '90s, we started seeing less and less *local business* activities. For a while, we wondered what was happening and decided to research it. We found that as budgets were cut, more and more people were fired. With so many people experiencing layoffs, workplace friendships suffered. People lost their friends at work due to these layoffs or downsizing. It became hard for these people to remain focused on their work or follow through with their friendly nature. They became demotivated and disengaged. It became hard for new people in the workplace to fit in and be a part of the workforce. The new employees were as disengaged as the old ones.

- If this blow wasn't enough, the information highway came along, and BAM! People's free time seemed to disappear. No longer were people free for their co-workers anymore, partly due to the lack of friends at work and partly due to technology.

- During the year 1990, if you invited the department to go bowling on Friday after work, 90% of the people would go. By 1995, however, the numbers decreased, and only 50% would agree to a game night or a fun evening with co-workers. Inevitably, by 2000, the number dropped even more and people began to refuse company activities, saying it wasn't worth their time. Although recreational picnics were popular, things were starting to come to an end after these budget cuts. It all came to a halt because the employees who weren't laid off stood up for their friends and argued that the whole point of laying people off was to make a budget cut, which wasn't really happening with these recreational activities that were being planned and financed. The other popular reason to say no to these outings was that the employees missed having friends from work who would make the time invested enjoyable for them.

- As the decade of the '90s progressed, so started the trend of *fewer friends at work* and *more stress at work*. As technology became popular and eventually became the trend of the 2000s, people stopped having spare time. People became so used to the comfort or ease of work provided to them by their screens that they got stuck behind them. Most people realized that they were getting overwhelmed with faxes (remember them?), emails, and other methods of internal office communication. People started thinking to themselves, "If I go bowling, then I will have all these emails to get to when I come back from that or even worse. I will have to finish this work on Saturday morning!" For these reasons, they began to decline invitations to any activities that would help them bond with their co-workers.

- Remember, the data we just gave you was before the great market crash of 2008. So, we all get a picture of what things are like. People are extremely stressed out and equally busy today to have a fun time. Park and recreate is the best way to avert that stress and turn the whole mess into a happier life for the employees. That way, employees come to work happy, do their work happily, and leave happy.

Let's look at how you might be able to Park and Recreate with your team.

As expert recreation programmers, we understand what activities are the best to experience, connect with one another, have fun, stay involved, and value the time together. Just having happy hours, catered lunches and snacks, or a Ping-Pong table isn't the solution to a happy workplace. The solution is simpler than this view of fun.

Besides monthly workouts, quality quarterly experiences are a way out of this struggle for you and your group of co-workers. Focusing on activities that can bring the team together every once in a while can really help your group. The frequency and the quality of time spent are the keys to that. There is another thing; however, that is even more important than these two factors. It's the attitude of the employee. You can have thousands of these recreational activities, but they will be of no avail if the attitude of the worker isn't right. This leads us back to our team workouts and team talk. These two give the team time to be together. They help to create a bond of friendship or, at the very least, a sense of connection amongst the workforce.

Team time can go two ways, negative and positive.

Team Time Gone Negatively

This creates an unhappy attitude chain, which is leaving for work unhappy and going home unhappy. This fills people with dread for the upcoming team time and recreational activity. They think of it as a chore. Just another task added to their pile of work tasks. They begin to view it as something unworthy of their time. This may sound like a little thing, but this bad attitude gets transferred to group outings, employee birthday celebrations, or worse, the meetings.

A meeting can lose its entire purpose due to such an attitude. Two-way conversation is needed for various reasons, but if avoided, it creates disengagement amongst other disadvantages. All of these have a direct impact on the performance and the revenue of the business.

Team Time Gone Positively

This creates a happy attitude chain. Employees leave work happy. They go home happy. They leave from home and for work happy. If the employees can bond well, they will establish friendships and will already be halfway through an engaging and fun environment. This has certain benefits that greatly help business progress. People look forward to any group activities that come along, be it birthdays, group outings, planning sessions, or, most importantly, meetings. They feel thoroughly engaged, and so they engage in all sorts of positive communications in all these activities. They find these experiences to be meaningful and worthy of their time.

This is why the importance of creating and staying in a positive, engaging work environment has been emphasized throughout the book. This chain of happiness boosts our work lives. It also ensures that our personal lives are happy and that we properly divide our time between work, home, and ourselves.

Fun at work established through meaningful time as a team will create an environment where people are willing to do things away from work together. Todd was asked by a high-level executive about his opinion of bosses or supervisors going out with the team during their off work hours.

After mulling over the question, he responded with, *"I think it is great if people want to go!"* Because we know people who are forced become part of the negative or unhappy team, which is not good for the person and the company.

Adding to the conversation, Todd asked, *"Are you assuming they want to go to happy hour, drink, or do they want to go play volleyball, hike, or volunteer?"*

The manager thought and then said, *"Oh, I get what you are saying."* People want to go, and where we go and what we do add value to the experience and the team.

This was the answer given by a top manager. Why do we forget to stop and unwind? Secondly, why do we think that making time to Park (or stop), Recreate (or unwind), and have fun has to be around a bar? Why do we think it needs to involve drinking? Now we don't have a problem with a group going out to the pub and socializing done safely. But if we are trying to build a team, there are plenty of fun activities to do that can be more rewarding.

Drinking isn't an inclusive activity and only works for a while. We want something more. We want something more inclusive and long-lasting. Why not *earn and burn your calories* or make it a heartfelt cause for a more inclusive experience. This is why we suggest that quarterly quality time for outings is a positive way to relax your team. This is also easier to plan, and people look forward to the quarterly outing, celebration, and having some fun.

Here Are Some Tips to Remember with Group Outings

Competitive outings can be fun if they are planned well and executed perfectly and with design. Ideally, a perfect plan allows all abilities and all sorts of employees to participate. A well-executed plan engages all these participants.

It is a fun activity that includes all abilities. Have you ever gone bowling for two and a half hours? Do you know that most people struggle at bowling? Try team bowling where you can eat lunch and play five fun team games in one and a half hours. You can now see your co-workers in another setting, learn about them, and knock down walls. Change the way you play, where you use an alternative player roll, so the game moves faster with a team, not individual score. This will make it competitive enough so that everyone wants to participate but friendly enough for the average bowlers to feel included in the fun. This will make sure that the *bad bowlers* don't look so bad. This can also be applied to Top Golf or even a nine-hole golf outing. Try to do grouping versus individual tokens for play. Group play is more rewarding and helps relationship building. If you want to play volleyball without people getting hurt and have competition, play recreation rules in volleyball. No blocking, no spiking, and two hits minimum before going back over the net. It requires teamwork and reduces the chances of an injury. As with anything, you can twist an ankle while playing.

These are the activity samples that we find useful. Remember, it can be anything as long as all participants feel positive and engaged. The important thing to remember is to include everyone so that everyone has fun away from work and then later back at work.

Note: For more fun, engaging, and recreational activities, check out www.parkandrecreate.com.

Time is everything. When you take a group out for fun, it is necessary to ensure that they do not feel like their time is wasted. This can result in a negative outcome of team time. As shared with bowling, see how you can get your inclusive, fun activity done and enjoyed within two to three hours at maximum. From our experiences, we have noticed two hours of team time is the best as people tend to enjoy and value it more.

Volunteering is our top suggested group outing for people to connect, share the experience, and give back to the community. This is the one area of recreation that people look forward to and share fond memories after the experience. Remember, volunteering is a healthy way to get others involved. By giving back to the community and helping others, they are essentially putting a smile on someone's face. A smile is contagious. It spreads around, making the volunteers happy and establishing the chain of happiness.

Volunteering that uses creativity as part of the experience is the best way to give back as it allows people to work together to complete a project. We created the concept of VolunTEAMism. It is the best and most rewarding of all methods as you share the start and finish to feel a sense of accomplishment. Creating self-organized volunteer clubs is a great suggestion for any organization, allowing people to choose and give time to their cause. They allow people to connect on their own time to give back to the community. Using a company outing as a way to motivate groups to volunteer on their own time is another beneficial aspect of all this. In fact, it can lead to run and walk clubs being formed to participate in events on a monthly basis as opposed to a quarterly basis. This is because people feel that their time is valued, and so they want to engage in the activity more frequently.

Note: Check out www.volunteamism.com for more ideas on how to bring your employees together to give back to the community.

In 2002, we started a new brand called Fun Coach Team Workouts (www.funcoachusa.com). Our first project was with an engineering client who felt that their office team was disconnected. He asked what he could do about it and how we could help. We designed 'the 24-hour makeover project' for the solution to his challenges. This allowed quality time in which we played, talked, and recreated. Throughout the planned, purpose-driven, problem-solving, and fun activities that spanned over three Fridays, we were able to change the culture of the company successfully. Results hinted at the fact that since people valued their time together, they felt more comfortable approaching others during the workday to achieve business goals. This made work even more rewarding as people realized their need for recreation and activities away from work to be less stressed on these occasions. After this activity, employees began experimenting on their own by organizing their own "fun Fridays."

Since then, with Marsha's guidance, we have perfected the work-leisure life balance program. See, life includes work and home life. Leisure time is made up of what we have to do in our free time or what sparks our interest. In the next chapter, we will discuss exactly why you need to be balanced and come to work happy and why it is important to have fun in all areas of life. This will improve your attitude and style, which in turn will help engage your entire team as you set the example for them.

Chapter 5: Fun Away from Work

Hobby: An enjoyable activity done regularly by an individual in their free time.

Synonyms include pastime, leisure, relaxation, interest, and leisure pursuit.

When was the last time you had time to indulge yourself in an activity that you enjoy? When was the last time you took time out to do what you like, for example, paint or hike? Previously, we discussed the chain of happiness and the idea that if we're happy at work, we will be happy at home too. This goes both ways. To be happy at work, we need to be happy away from work too. We need to invest time in our personal lives. We need to balance our lives with our workload and leisure time to live a happier, healthier, and productive life. This means having fun away from work is just as important as having fun at work. Marsha has been our champion and program designer for this project. We have found people who enjoy life and are happier all day long.

Our objective has always been to help individuals find life balance. This chapter aims to guide you to hit that goal. The main focus of this chapter, however, is *you*. As a human, as an individual, and as a manager, it is a matter of great importance that you take time out for yourself. Time to recreate. Time to immerse yourself in your interests and hobbies. You need to spend your time doing what *you* like.

Contentment from one's personal life results in happiness, friendliness, and satisfaction in both personal and professional lives. We have observed and learned this from our workshop experiences. People who take time out for themselves are happy and satisfied with their personal lives. Therefore, they are more engaged. This state of life reflects positively in their work lives. This is why life balance has become an important value that we teach everyone and call this having fun away from work.

The Phenomenon of Life Balance

Listening to the responses of executives who were our participants in fun workshops led us to start Fun Coach USA in the first place. We soon began to realize that most people connected with and understood our teachings. They recognized that their lack of play or fun time impacted their attitude at work and kept them from being there or present at work and home. Simply teaching people about the philosophy wasn't enough. We wanted to do more than that and help people discover and implement a healthy work-life balance. So we designed a workshop called "Get A Life Have More Fun."

Over the past 20 years, we have been facilitating work-leisure life balance workshops for companies. While listening to participants, we discovered important values to share with you all. We found that only three out of ten people were happy or satisfied with their jobs and personal lives. These three people were the same who took time out for themselves away from work. They invested time in their interests constantly and consistently to do their hobbies and volunteer work. They did what made them happy. They carried out different activities that ensured the well-being of their physical, spiritual, and emotional states.

The remaining seven out of ten were those who struggled at work. Work-life suffered due to their attitude and fear of missing out. The majority admitted that they either didn't have the time or weren't taking time out for themselves. The workload was the same for all of these ten people, but the habits, attitudes, and productivity differed for all of them simply because three people were taking time out weekly to enjoy themselves as opposed to the others. Granted, there are many life situations that keep people busy and add stress, but we discovered that those who made time for their interests were happier at work.

These three people were successful. They were the ones who managed to strike a feeling of balance in life. You strive to find a work-life balance, but you struggle or never get there. Ask yourself, what are we balancing? Time at work? Time sleeping? Time doing home projects? If you sleep 56 hours a week, do you spend the same time with your closest friends or hobbies? If you work 50 hours a week, can you spend that same amount of time on your closest relationships? The answer is no. This is why there is no accurate measure of balance when measured with time.

Our life is so full of obligations and expectations. We begin to prefer them to our leisure time. It is important to realize that finding balance is not a measurement or time factor. The deciding factor is integration. It is the goal to find a sense of balance, better well-being, and a feeling that one is living life with interest. You don't have to give 50 hours a week to yourself to find or maintain the balance. All you have to do is do something you like. Take the luxury of immersing in your hobbies, even if it's for a short time. It will make you feel that you did something worthwhile. It will rejuvenate you and lift your spirit.

You're probably wondering what these interests are. You have been involved in your work-life so deeply that you've lost touch with your personal life. There are many social, emotional, and physical activities that you can do. Not only do we teach you to bring back your life balance, but we also teach activities that will assist in achieving that goal. We teach and preach that we all owe ourselves time to do what we are passionate about. We all should have a life outside work and desire to make our personal life healthy and fun too.

All of us have an *obligated time* during the week. It is the time when we work. We do our duties at and away from work. During this time, we do our chores and fulfill our responsibilities – professional and personal both. Once we have completed all these tasks, we have our *free time,* which we call leisure time. It is the key to our emotional and physical well-being. This is where the fun begins and spreads from. Choose your hobby. Choose what you want to do. Prioritize your life leisure balance. Look past your obligations and do what interests you.

Give yourself time to reflect on your personal life. Give time to your relationships. If you have a family, spend quality time with them. Invest in fun time with your spouse or significant other. Spend some positive time with your friends. Constantly working is tough on you, and taking a healthy break from the hectic schedule allows you to bring balance back into your life. Make memories with your loved ones so that you aren't just remembered by your friends and family as someone who overworked and quit being fun. Your work is important, but so are your relationships and having a social life healthy and important for you. Investing time in interests can be a challenge in the age of entertainment on demand. There is no such term as *too much screen time* in our dictionary because we see it as a form of recreation. It's a source of stress reduction. Unplugging from too much screen time and engaging in wellness, which includes physical, spiritual, and emotional activities, is a challenge for almost everyone. If you spend ten hours of the week watching your interests on tv, then we recommend taking at least the same time and dedicating it to your other interests.

There are several types of interests that people can invest time in. Time spent weekly and monthly can be part of the integration into life. These are:

Physical

Remember that a *body at rest stays at rest*. Keeping your body active reinforces the value that a *body in motion stays in motion*. It also keeps you fit, healthy, and happy. Physical can be working out at the gym, biking, hiking, running, walking, and playing sports, and can be shared with others to provide social connections. Walking the mall briskly and stopping to make a purchase might be considered physical, but this can be tricky as it may be heavy on the pocket.

Emotional

Participating in the activities that rejuvenate our spirit and soul are the ones that ensure our emotional well-being. If you like music, write or sing. If you like arts, paint, draw, or tour museums. If you're interested in the theater, act or attend shows. If you like to volunteer, serve where you are interested to give back to the community. If you are intrigued by the outdoors, walk, hike, visit a beach, or bike. Outdoors is one area that restores our bodies through reflections, clean air, views, and adventures. It always has a calming effect on us.

Spiritual

If you have a spiritual side, make and take time for your specific beliefs, interests, or paths in life. Spiritual can also be found in small groups, nature, meditation, and exercise programs like yoga. Combine yoga, quiet time, and exercise together, and you will meet spiritual, physical, and emotional wellness.

Social

Doing things with people makes spending the time much better. We call this shared time. Include a friend or family member in your hobbies. Look forward to connecting with people.

6 Fun Ways to Integrate into Your Life-Leisure Balance

You can get back to that feeling of play by practicing the methods of the *park* and *recreate* for your self-development. Previously, we focused on Park and Recreate as a team. Now you should practice this as an individual. To park means to shut off your engine, quit thinking or stressing over things, pause, and stop in your busy schedule of life. Recreate means to renew, restore, and reschedule intentional activities and interests to have fun. Our goal for individuals is to encourage them to invest time in hobbies, interests, fitness, friends, community, and personal values. Living in balance with your physical, spiritual, and emotional needs will help you look forward to life daily and weekly. Remember, as a manager or supervisor, you set the attitude for your team. You can encourage and motivate people to enjoy more of their interests without being too nosy or violating the HR world of restrictions. This may feel like another list of activities to add to your to-do list, but it's not. These activities aren't some mundane tasks that you are obligated to do. They are your escape from the stressful work life. They make life better for you step by step and like a ripple. This positivity and happiness spread to all aspects of your life. They ensure your physical and mental health and make your life enjoyable at and away from work.

Below is a list of leisure time pursuits that, when integrated, will help you maintain your work life.

Be Fit

The foundation of fun is based on your ability to stay energized to achieve all your goals in life. Whether you are at a gym or walking for 45 minutes in a park, you need three workouts a week of 45 to 60 minutes to keep your physical well-being up and running. Trainers and nutritionists often recommend this to stay fit. This can be a personal development goal or something you can prioritize for yourself. If you are a social person, find some friends to join and keep you motivated. Once you get in shape, enter fun runs and charity events to combine fit and fun with volunteering.

Volunteer

A key area of emotional well-being is volunteering. When you make and take time to serve and give, you have more fun in life. You may also make new friends who are engaged in community service. Volunteer and help people and animals. You can also serve professionally. These activities are all part of improving your emotional well-being. They allow you to serve the community which is the most satisfying experience one can ever have. Looking forward to your commitment is the secret to going back the next time.

Outdoors & Recreation

There are a variety of recreational experiences offered through local municipal agencies, nonprofits, and for-profit companies. These could include sports leagues, swimming programs, dance classes, pickleball, softball, dance, tennis, or volleyball, to name a few. The possibilities are endless. Challenge people from work to a monthly after-work or a weekend challenge. Put together a group and golf in charity events, and you will fulfill community and recreation in one outing. Find your outdoors and hike, bike, ski, fish, camp, and fill your emotional bucket up with the sun, wind, water, and fun while restoring your spirit. Check out your local parks, recreation department, and YMCA or meet up adventure groups.

Discover a Hobby

Also known as special interests, collecting, crafts, painting, pottery, and a variety of other activities are available to you and your friends. Hobbies can be something you do on your own as they can be different for all individuals or something you do with a group as finding people with common interests and hobbies isn't that difficult. This area of recreation helps you explore yourself. You delve further into your creative side. You can get rid of the stress accumulated in your life through creativity. It greatly improves your emotional well-being. Shopping is not a hobby. Okay, maybe that is debatable, but in my (Todd's) opinion, hunting and collecting antiques or yard sales might qualify as a hobby but collecting shoes, um, not so much! Check out your local parks, recreation department, and YMCA or meet up interest groups to experience old and new hobbies with other people.

Attend Special Events

What's going on in your backyard? In your state? Share mutual interests and schedule time to go to your favorite concert, art festival, car show, or other unique interests. This can be a great way to chill out, relax, or explore your hobbies and passion. When you go, put away the phone. Just enjoy the experience and the people you are with, if you can. Are you seeing the art, hearing the music, or just listening to the bling going off on your phone? Checking sports may be okay, well, or maybe not!

Travel

Day, weekend, or longer trips all provide a new perspective in life. Making and taking time can fit almost all budgets. They are the most effective way to rejuvenate oneself. Many people seem too busy to take vacations, yet you should plan one every year. Scheduling one or two-day trips once a month will help you look forward to getting away from the grind. Anytime you can combine interests with a travel trip. With an interest such as running at the beach, it will give your experience more value for the time and money invested. Fit it into your budget, and you will see for yourself that the rewards are priceless. Will you take a two-week vacation every year or maybe ten different three-day weekend trips? Have you heard of voluntourism? Look it up and plan a trip to build a house, dig a well, or find and help the cause of your choice.

Self-Time Test

We discovered the secret to happy people was based on the time they spent doing the things of interest and integrating consistently. People who come to work happy leave happy. There are 168 hours in a week. Decide what you will do with them and then look forward to your time doing what makes you restore, renew, and replenish your new life batteries. What do you do with your time weekly? See how this simple self-test of time plays out.

Here is a simple math calculation test for you. Check your score now and see how your time spent looks to you.

How many hours a week do you?

a. Sleep ______

b. Work ______

c. Do home projects ______

Total ______

Hours left from 168: _____ (subtract the total from 168)

How much time do you spend weekly on?

a) Physical well-being _____

b) Emotional well-being _____

c) Spiritual well-being _____

d) Social well-being _____

Total _____

If you feel low for time invested in yourself, what would you want to do with your time, more or less, to keep your life better balanced between projects and leisure time fun?

Check out www.ParkandRecreate.com for a life leisure checklist form.

If you are a manager or supervisor and you are not happy when you come to work, things will be hard for you and your entire workforce. You either are happy or aren't. There's no other answer to this. There's no way you can fake it. Understand that it can be tough to create the desired, friendly environment for others, if you struggle and discover that the change must come from within you. This may be cliché, but Gandhi said, "Be the change you want to see in the world." This is something that applies to your life as well.

As we teach, you can't be frustrated and uptight all day at work and think you can go home and turn on the happy switch for what matters most. It has to be the same all over. People who are active with their interests tend to be happier and more balanced in life. People who say they wish they had more time for their interests carry the most stress because they recognize the need to do things but never find the right time to do them. Our goal is to help you, as an individual, to find the time, then make time to integrate interests weekly.

If you have children of all ages, walk the park, hike, bike, review a movie, play video games, and engage them in meaningful conversations. When you create lifelong habits and interests, they will continue to enjoy these activities with you. Hike with someone for life. Golf with someone for life. Volunteer with someone for life. We call this lifestyle *living with interests*.

If you need friend time, walk the park, hike, or bike with them. Do whatever makes you happy. Find that social connection. As we like to say, "Share your time" with interests and friends, including family and close relationships.

Your personal life is as important as your work life. Stop neglecting that for your workload. Working overtime or staying late occasionally is acceptable and understandable. But, making it a habit is unhealthy and damaging in the long run. Apart from your friends and family, you need to make and take healthy time for yourself too. You are a manager, you have a busy schedule, and your life is challenging. Make time out for your interests. Watch what happens then. See how it makes you happy. Observe how it positively affects you and others around you. Don't just take our word for it. Try it! You owe yourself that much. Wouldn't you enjoy comments from staff saying our boss is so balanced and energetic?

Chapter 6: Be a Fun Coach Leader

An excellent leader: A person who has mastered the art of incorporating fun in their lifestyles and of their employees.

Synonyms include a top-level manager, a person who understands and values the importance of fun at and away from work, you, etc.

An excellent leader is one who makes an effort to make their work environment a fun place to be and work. Such leaders value the well-being of their employees and their company. They do their best to incorporate the values of fun at work and away from work. Now that you have learned all about fun at work and away from work, you will understand its importance too. The previous chapter was about fun away from work and showed how these two concepts are interrelated. These values are beneficial for you and your team. We have revealed our strategies and exercises, but that isn't enough.

You need to become a good facilitator to be able to incorporate these two useful techniques in your work environment successfully. The best part about it is that out of all the methods we teach, this one is the most rewarding. It is an easy process but takes thought and action to become a person who engages their employees, creates passion in their hearts, and helps people find purpose at and away from their job.

The reason why we say this is rewarding is that our job is pretty much the same. Marsha and I are fun event managers and facilitators, and we love what we do. Of course, our work revolves around creating *fun* for others, so that is pretty much obvious. The thing is, this is an easy job, and so anyone can become a fun facilitator. For us, the vision and inspiration for fun all started from our experiences and a training program called Fish.

Fish for Fun!

Well, it's not what you are thinking right now. We aren't talking about actual fishing, even though Todd's favorite lifetime hobby is fly fishing. We are talking about the world-famous fish market in Seattle. Again, it's not what you are thinking. We are not talking about creepy, smelly, dead fish staring at you. We aren't talking about smelly people serving and selling fish. We are talking about something beyond the stereotypes. We are talking about a truth that revolutionized the fun industry for corporate America, right around the end of the '90s and going into the millennium. Perfect timing!

Twenty years ago, Todd became a teacher of the Fish Philosophy based on the Pikes Fish Market in Seattle. This is a story about a difficult work culture transforming into a fun place for all employees and customers. The fish market represents an engaged and fun environment where everyone, from customers to workers, was enjoying themselves. This gave the protagonist of the story, who had recently become a manager, the inspiration to incorporate fun at work to produce a similar, friendly work environment. This process created a foundation on how to improve the quality of work life by the team members of the market.

Four important beliefs were discussed in the teaching process. We like to include these core values in our teachings to help managers and employers become the best at their jobs and encourage others to do the same. These values allow workers to enjoy what they do and make them look forward to the next day. These values are all interconnected and include:

Play

This probably seems out of place because playing and working are two contradicting terms. However, this simply means engaging activities at work such as Team Play, Team Time, and Team Workouts. These activities involving Play are not a hindrance to your productivity, nor do they affect your team's work. All of these activities only improve the quantity and quality of work that you and your team do. They help bring your team together, increase productivity, and elevate your mood, which helps you choose a better attitude at work.

Be There

As a manager, it is important to value time with your team members and make them feel included and engaged in the business processes. It is important to give attention individually and as a team. This may seem impossible with your current workload; however, being there for your fellow co-workers is a great way to boost morale and loyalty. It can be made possible by Team Talk, which is the best way to be there for everyone.

As an employer or manager, it is equally important to value your customers and give them attention. You don't only have to be there physically, but you also have to be present mentally and emotionally. A good manager is capable of understanding what their customers require. They are quick on their feet, make fast decisions, and always deliver what the customer wants. This gains brand loyalty and enhances business. Company and customers aside, great managers practice these habits for themselves. It brings meaning to their interactions with the customers and makes them *love what they do.*

Make Their Day

This is a combination of the two points mentioned above, by including customers and employees both in your play. By doing this, you spread positivity all around. It makes it memorable and you make their day. You provide them with an experience they have never seen or felt before. It increases the value of your company. Simple practices make the experience worthwhile for you, your workers, and your customers. Team Workouts are one of the best ways to do just that.

Choose Your Attitude

Your attitude is a choice, isn't it? You get to pick whether you wish to go to work happily or unhappily and whether you stay in the state you choose to go in or not. You have the power to choose and decide. Keep in mind that whatever mood you take along with you at work, your employees and co-workers will observe and pick up on it too. This will be followed by the customers as well. If you cross the street and see someone smiling at you, the response is automatic. You smile back at them. It's the same if you see someone with a frown. Your attitude is contagious, so make a choice to bring one with you to work.

After teaching these four values and listening to feedback from participants, we realized that the relationship between these values runs deeper than we initially thought it to be. The truth is that you can't *choose your attitude* unless you take time to play, have fun, and, as we say, "Park and Recreate." In 2002, we created the Fun Coach brand with the vision that the business plan would help bring fun back to a work team. As previously mentioned, by then, the idea of fun at work had become a rare phenomenon. It was from there that we realized people weren't having fun at work as they became busier and busier with a sense of urgency. Added to that, there was the fact that 70% of people were saying they weren't having fun away from work.

All of this made us realize the importance of a Fun Coach. As much as a business needs capital, business coaches, and good employees to function, we knew then that employers really needed a fun coach for their business to thrive. The mission was to change the way people viewed their co-workers and to motivate them to find their source of fun away from work. This theory proved to be correct. From all of our sessions conducted in the past, Fun at and Away from Work just worked. It put the responsibility back on all the participants to value co-workers and restore fun to their personal life.

If you want to be a fun facilitator, here is a challenge for you. You have to follow three steps, and that's it. Yes, you heard it right! It can happen easily in three basic steps. These steps are:

Step 1: Take 30 days to integrate fun away from work in your life and see how your life changes. Schedule physical, spiritual, and emotional interest time, and you will be ready to come to work happy. Be deliberate and integrate them into your schedule.

Step 2: After these 30 days, when you have *refreshed* yourself and seem more natural in your ways, introduce Team Talk to your team members. Create engagement in your group by using the Team Talk principles and guidelines. You may want to practice with some friends or associates away from work to feel comfortable with the process.

Step 3: Implement a monthly *problem-solving* program for which we always use the Team Talk method. Then it is time to turn to the Team Workouts. Apart from that, add a quarterly activity for your staff to keep them engaged in a fun environment through Team Play or VolunTEAMism method. Remember, the conversation makes the time invested worth it to your team.

Yep, that's it. So, do you have it in you to be a fun coach manager, supervisor, or board member? Are you willing to become the best manager?

Do You Want More Help?

Apart from this, we also offer a certification program so that you can become a certified fun coach. Obviously, if you want to be a fun coach, it's better to be taught by a teacher and trained by fun people with 30 plus years of experience in the same field.

Certification Program

Having fun at work is beneficial for various reasons. Let's recognize fun isn't PING PONG at work, a luncheon, a birthday party, or a bowling event. None of this sparks a connection amongst the team members. To have fun at work, we need to think differently. The idea is that this is a process that creates a consistent team approach to fun, communication, teamwork, and doing what you get paid to do! We have given you all the elements of being an engaging manager or supervisor for a company or even a committee, board, or group. We have provided teaching and training for years, and this book is to provide information, techniques, and goals for you to have more fun at and away from work. But we know how addictive and rewarding being a fun facilitator can be. This is why we have decided to do more than that.

Starting this year, we have started a *certificate* program. Here, we will teach and train individuals to utilize Team Workouts, Team Talk, and Team Play and encourage work-life leisure balance within their company. Basically, it will be more practical and detailed teaching. As a fun coach, you will learn how to be engaging. You will be taught how to use a consistent process (that is also beneficial) for your organization. Furthermore, you can learn new ideas or solutions designed especially for your workplace. We are writing this amid the COVID-19 crisis and creating new ideas on how distance and technical solutions work together to build all these qualities in an organization.

Teaching Team Values

"Without the environment of FUN at work, the values of the team won't happen!"

This is the motto that we live by. We offer a more in-depth and unique training approach to the values of spending time together as a work team. We aim to get the team members together so that they can come together and be involved in planning, performing, and building a sense of friendship among co-workers.

TEAM or, as we mentioned previously, Together Everyone Achieves More values will demonstrate for participants how their individual needs must be met. Three elements of a healthy team will be presented and combined with the value of the *I* in team or individual and their attitude they bring to work (FISH). Individuals will be challenged to embrace an attitude and accept a lifestyle of fun at work while integrating time for fun away from work.

For fun at work, this is our acronym that you should learn, memorize, and live by.

F*riendships*

U*nity*

N*eeds*

A sense of **F**riendship or consideration of others is the first and most important value of **FUN**. When people feel connected to the team or that they are part of the group, then **U**nity will happen more naturally. The bottom line is the **N** of FUN or the **N**eeds will be met for the individual once Friendship and Unity come to fruition. These needs include feeling valued and the achievements of the organization.

Being a fun coach is not that hard. All it requires is for you to follow three steps with consistency. Always remember that you must live fun to be fun. To be authentic and to value people and their productivity, fun is an important value that you must incorporate in your life first and then in your team members. Yes, we all play to win, but being fun keeps the team performing and being intact longer. You will learn a process, and these core values of FUN and TEAM Talk, TEAM Play, TEAM Workouts, and Life-leisure balance will all be included in your training in the most fun way possible.

Chapter 7: Be a Facilitator Leader

Facilitator: A person or leader who makes an action or process easy or easier. According to Webster, a facilitator is someone who helps bring about an outcome (such as learning, productivity, or communication) by providing indirect or unobtrusive assistance, guidance, or supervision.

Example: A true educator acts as a facilitator of learning

A good leader is one who works to make their work environment fun. They engage their employees as much as they can. But an excellent leader is one who can be a facilitator leader. They are the ones who achieve success every step of the way. Being a facilitator is a trait that sets apart a good manager from an excellent one.

Everyone has a different style of leadership. Our goal isn't to change your style of supervision to something it isn't. There are many different styles of managers, leaders, and supervisors. We believe everyone can become a good facilitator leader when it comes to strategic planning and team meetings. Our focus in one of the upcoming sections will be on the styles of leadership. This section, however, is on the *team* of any organization where an individual manages or influences teamwork through information sharing and the dreaded *meetings*.

Why are meetings so dreaded? Is it the manager who resists these meetings because they have to lead them? Or is it the employees who dread another staff meeting? Could it be because everyone feels there are far more important things to do with their time?

Pay attention to these findings of an interesting report conducted by Doodle[5] here. According to Doodle's 2019 State of Meetings report, the cost of poorly organized meetings in 2019 will reach about $399 billion in the U.S. and $58 billion in the U.K. This is almost half a trillion dollars for these two

---

[5] The State of Meeting Reports 2019. Doodle. Retrieved from https://meeting-report.com/

countries alone. The findings predict huge costs and a tremendous drag on the effectiveness of businesses. This is only the financial side of the burden. The other party that suffers is the employees because they are forced to sit through the meetings. The report also reveals some of the consequences for employees who suffer from poorly organized meetings.

- Poorly organized meetings mean I don't have enough time to do the rest of my work (44 percent).
- Unclear words and actions lead to confusion (43 percent).
- Bad organization results in a loss of focus on projects (38 percent).
- Irrelevant attendees slow down the progress (31 percent).
- Inefficient processes weaken client/supplier relationships (26 percent).

This isn't all. Being in this industry for so long has given us exposure to many meetings that support such reports and statistics, including one that revealed close to 70% of the employees wanted better communication at work. They mentioned that communication didn't need to be written but verbal or in person. Even though people wanted this human *communication time*, the problem remained. When it came down to executing this, seven out of ten people didn't look forward to the meeting and felt the meeting was a waste of time. You can see from the Doodle report; there were a lot of reasons behind the lack of interest in these meetings. Since no quality time or discussion was being spent or done in these meetings, most of the people didn't look forward to it. The need for quality human interaction is actually what is lacking in problematic workplaces. This is what creates a good meeting. It is just that simple.

Since everyone can't be the *perfect* communicator or team leader of human meetings, as shared in Chapter 3, Team Talk is a solution that works for almost everyone. Once you learn to use Team Talk, you can move on to Team Workouts. This will let you create a healthy interactive team through problem-solving. Team Workouts allow practicing behaviors that also turn into work-related skills for strategic conversations.

So remember, when seven out of ten people wanted a better meeting, they actually thought that the meeting was a waste of time and they deserved to spend their time in a better, more meaningful way. The confusion that surrounds all this is that, is it the delivery of the meeting, the content, or the personality of the host that affects the quality time and compromises the importance of the meeting? Over the years, we have recognized that about seven out of ten people are somewhat or very out of balance. They are the ones who want something, but then when they have it, they don't value it because they are out of time and can't appreciate the time invested. So, as important as the team workout, team talk, and fun away from work are, the style in which you deliver the experience matters too.

Types of Team Meetings

There are many different types of meetings conducted. Information is shared in multiple ways. We have broken down the team meetings into the three most common styles.

Brainstorming

In these types of meetings, new ideas are encouraged. These meetings are open for everyone to participate in. The idea behind this is that any individual or any idea could lead to an *input* discussion on every suggestion. Brainstorming is a good style to use. Then take the ideas and move them into *team talk* round table, facilitator-led discussions. With a team that feels free to share, progress is guaranteed.

We also like to use the *popcorn* style sharing method where people just pop out their ideas in no particular order but sharing as needed. There is no time given to deliberate over the *pop*. Instead, each pop should be accompanied by a paper tossed into the middle of the table with their pop idea on the card. If you want to have fun, you can give everyone a set quantity of popcorn in a bowl, and they can only share that many times. This forces people to think a bit before they pop.

Brainstorm is fast and furious, where popcorn may be more thought-driven. It is as simple as, "I am thinking of painting our break room. What color do you think would be best..." Brainstorming is done for multiple ideas that do not require any deep thought.

Information Sharing

In these meetings, the required information is provided without discussion. This is more of a fact-sharing kind of meeting and requires some feedback for clarification. This feedback can be received in many ways. It can be verbal or written, which can be taken in the form of a survey, test, or other forms. For this, Team Talk would be a fast way to facilitate questions on *information*. You may provide information and then call on each person to share what they perceive or hear, so they will hear answers from others.

If you set the agenda, start with sharing information, and then close with a topic with you becoming a participant too, in the very end, this will engage the group. Let's say you want to paint the room blue. Information may be, let's say, based on our last popcorn sharing session, it seemed blue was the color most desired for the room. Here are some shades of blue to review. When we go around the room, share your shade with the reason why you like it. Now you just got people involved.

Now, we want more input and feeling into that feedback.

Input Meeting

This is a discussion-based meeting that focuses on getting individual ideas and input on a topic or a series of topics that could lead to further action, meeting, or group consensus. This requires a facilitator host to guide the process. It may be the manager, a non-team member, or anyone who has been trained in the process. Always remember; a process only works well when it is done consistently. Team Talk was developed to provide positive meeting engagement by all through a quick process designed to provide a solution-driven interactive team environment.

Effective Leadership Styles

As promised, here are some leadership styles as described in Wise Toast which is worth your time to read. We will use three styles of leadership published in Wise Toast[6] to help participants discover where they might fit in based on the role of supervision they play. The 12 leadership styles are:

1. Autocratic leadership
2. Democratic leadership
3. Strategic leadership
4. Transformational leadership
5. Team leadership
6. Cross-cultural leadership
7. Facilitative leadership
8. Laissez-faire leadership
9. Transactional leadership
10. Coaching leadership
11. Charismatic leadership
12. Visionary leadership

This was eye-opening for us as there are many different situations for leadership styles to be in place. For Team Leadership (point number 5), an

---

[6] (2020). 12 different types of leadership styles. Wise Toast. Retrieved from https://wisetoast.com/types-of-leadership-styles/

article follows our sentiments. TeamPlay is our business brand so let's see what the article says about TEAM (Together Everyone Achieves More) Leadership.

"TEAM LEADERSHIP: Team leadership involves the creation of a vivid picture of its future, where it is heading, and what it will stand for. The vision inspires and provides a strong sense of purpose and direction. Team leadership is about working with the hearts and minds of all those involved. It also recognizes that teamwork may not always involve trusting cooperative relationships. The most challenging aspect of this leadership is whether or not it will succeed. According to the Harvard Business Review, team leadership may fail because of poor leadership qualities."

In a world of flat organization charts, leadership at the manager level is one of the most challenging goals today. The biggest challenge is getting everyone together in time to achieve more. Forming a team and becoming engaged is one of the hardest things to do in today's modern and competitive business world. Team talk and leading through guiding is a great process to get your team on the same page as everyone, with the same vision.

We would also like to focus on point number 10, which features coaching leadership. As we are "The Fun Coaches," with our extensive background in the world of teams and players, we find this style the most effective. Marsha leads this charge as she has coached basketball teams for over 30 years. She incorporated these traits to build better team players, programs, and results.

About this type of leadership, the article states, *"Coaching leadership involves teaching and supervising followers. A coaching leader is highly operational in a setting where results/performances require improvement. Basically, in this kind of leadership, followers are helped to improve their skills. Coaching leadership does the following: motivates followers, inspires followers, and encourages followers."*

Two things have to happen for this coaching style to succeed. First, you need a good coach with experience and the ability to lead effectively. Have you ever had that coach or manager who when left, the next one in had a tough act to follow? The second point to remember is, you ought to have a team of players ready to engage in the process.

This entire chapter is about the art of being a facilitator, so of course, we will review facilitator leadership (point number 7). As per the article, *"Facilitative leadership is too dependent on measurements and outcomes – not a skill, although it takes much skill to master. The effectiveness of a group is directly related to the efficacy of its process. If the group is high functioning, the facilitative leader uses a light hand on the process. On the other hand, if the group is low-functioning, the facilitative leader will be more directive in helping the group run its process. Effective facilitative leadership involves monitoring of group dynamics, offering process suggestions and interventions to help the group stay on track."*

The interesting point of facilitative leadership is that the article states it to be, "Not a skill, although it takes much skill to master it." For this, the process itself is the key point. Without a process, you may have to depend on a personality, which can never meet the majority of a team's expectations. This is why we use Team Talk. It provides solutions with room for adjustments for both high- and low-functioning groups. Team Talk is one of the most important parts of being a facilitator, which is why the next section is devoted to it.

The Art of Facilitation for Workouts and Team Talk

Team Talk isn't the only beneficial tool for being a facilitator. Team Workouts are just as important. Let's talk about the art of facilitation and how it relates to these two methods. We want to keep it simple because you will become a facilitator for your team. You can take training classes to get better and become a facilitator for people outside your team too.

But for your purpose right now, you can just follow and implement a few easy techniques, which will help you become a facilitator. Not everything has to be facilitated, but if you want your team to be engaged and discover how they can implement a vision, even yours, then facilitation becomes a process that you would want to use. Facilitate your meetings using Team Talk, which is a style of facilitation. Facilitate your Team Workouts with Team Talk for solutions, and you will have a facilitative, coaching style of team leadership. You can also participate in discussions as long as you don't try to convince, sway, or influence the conversation. This is the reason why we recommend that the host gives their input at the end of the discussion. We believe leading through guiding means you are hired to provide direction to the team and talent.

Conversations need to have a direction. As you get good at this, they will go in the direction you want them to and will continue to provide desired solutions and outcomes. Becoming a good facilitator and incorporating Team Talk will allow you to start becoming a better team. Good facilitators do their homework and bring agenda items to discuss that can have real outcomes. This way, they can save time. Meetings without outcomes can be considered a waste of time for you and the team, which is what causes everyone to dread these meetings.

Remember, to be a good facilitator, you don't need to be an extrovert, introvert, controller, or kickback type of person. You just need to neutralize your personality and use the process like TEAM Talk. It will help you achieve your goals.

Let's use the full form of TEAM now to define keys to facilitating.

Together

Facilitation is about making people connect, communicate, and collaborate toward a common cause. All of this needs to be done in a fun and friendly way to encourage a healthy work environment. This is why Team Talk is recommended. It will make people feel together in the aspect of sharing.

Team Talk is good for groups with as few as three people and usually a maximum of eight. It is best to sit at different tables, or breakout chat rooms, with a designated host to lead and report back from the group to the head facilitator. We have successfully facilitated conversations with 16 tables, providing guidelines and rules of the table host at the start of the meeting.

Tips on Setting Up the Room

- Use round tables as much as possible or two rectangle tables
- 5-7 people at a table to keep conversations moving and effective
- In multiple tables, train a table host but guide the questions for consistency
- Consider having 45-minute sessions followed by a break and move people to new groups if desired

Everyone

A facilitator usually guides the process of a meeting. Remember, the process balances the talkers and the thinkers so that everyone can participate. You can trust anyone assigned to being a table host if they follow the process. When we use table hosts, we will go around and check in on the process and maybe suggest tips and adjustments during the first set of questions. If you have less than eight people, then one person can easily facilitate the whole group. If you have eight or more, you can divide them into two or more groups, according to what suits you. If you feel like switching people after a while, make sure they have at least three questions to discuss. Frequent switching can disconnect and disrupt the flow of the meeting which isn't what we want.

Achieves

The success of most meetings revolves around a basic fact. People feel a sense of achievement when they are heard. Spotlighting is a term we use when getting feedback from a group on their discussion. Spotlighting means, you listen first and then emphasize a point you heard that ties to the mission or goal of the meeting. This can be something that you believe needs to come out of the session and desire to have heard during the feedback.

With one to three tables, you can use the spotlighting method on one person at a time to share something that they can take back from the session(s). You can get through three tables pretty quickly if you use the process in a simple and to-the-point manner. This is a great time to reinforce the participant *ahas* or discoveries, value the team talk process, and connect the dots to *where you are going* or, as we say, leading through guiding the process.

When you have maybe four to eight tables, have each table host and ask their participants for feedback at the table without spotlighting. You would then ask each table host to share their table team discoveries with everyone. After that, spotlight what your table hosts share, as you will begin to hear similar comments from the table groups. The benefit of facilitator *spotlighting* is that the whole group gets to hear what other table groups discovered through their conversations.

More

So, if the bottom line to TEAM is *more*, what is the *more* of facilitation? You stress less about the presentation and get *more* out of the process. Then you get *more* people to participate, no matter their styles. This means you were *more* effective with the time you had your team invest in the meeting. You have *more* input that you can use for your leadership decisions and directions. Participants felt *more* engaged, involved, and valued because they had a chance to share and listen. Let's end the *more* section by saying that all these activities ought to be so much *more* valuable and fun than any other regular meeting.

Keys to Facilitation

Now that we have discussed facilitation in detail, here are our keys to the art of facilitation.

- Set up your tables or areas to fit the size of your audience into groups of 5-7.
- Explain the mission of Team Talk to every participant. Guide and ease them into the art of this style of conversation.
- Decide if the input on a subject is a light, medium, or deep conversation. For deeper conversations and discussion, use a path to get there eventually with your group.
- Give each topic a time limit. Both you and the participants will be amazed at how efficient Team Talk is for moving discussions consistently.
- Once everyone has shared their input on a specific point, you can open it up for additional comments and have people share as they feel necessary.
- With multiple groups and table hosts, have them wave at you or let you know in some other way when they have finished.
- Be a good listener and hear what is being said so you can be an effective spot-lighter.
- Put all your biases aside for people and ideas. For Team Talk to be successful, there should be no prejudice. Don't fight back on ideas. Embrace the value of individual input and remember the art of saying "Thank You" at the end of each idea.

Our Goal of Fun at Work: To Train You as a Facilitator

The goal of this book was to teach managers, supervisors, and volunteer team leaders how they can engage people in meaningful conversations and create positive human interaction. You can hire someone to come in and facilitate. You know people who put everything up on a chart, then type it up, and give it to you for $1,500 a day. Or you can learn to facilitate your meetings and bring respect back to your leadership, the way you conduct engagement to the participants, and the way you value teamwork.

It takes a good facilitator to understand the process of Team Talk, value the individual input and ideas, and then host the exchange in an open, trusting way. Remember, the manager who always says, "I want your feedback," and then the first person to say something is belittled or put aside. It can be through words as direct as "That's a terrible idea, I completely disagree" or something as subtle as, "Oh no, I am afraid that won't work as well as we want it to." Remember how that kind of manager is disliked by all? Do you want to be that kind of manager?

We have learned a few things over our careers. One of the most valuable lessons we have learned is, "When people share as a group and everyone has time to give input, great things are achieved." People learn more from listening to others, their perception, and their solutions to the question at hand. It helps them form their own opinions and give their intended input.

You have all been through a personality test that tries to tell you who you are, who you can be, and how you can improve. Well, don't get us going on that subject. Tests without authentic teamwork, trust, and respect can create labels and confusion. Personality tests can be effective when you have high-functioning teams with proper facilitation. Without trust, you can just create labels.

Leadership is a tough word to define, especially in today's professional world. Is it the C-suite executive? The business owner? The human resources department? The department manager or supervisor? There are tons of books on leadership. Some consider all of this information an overuse of the definition. We want you to consider the concept of leading through guiding people in a direction you need to go, but they feel as though they were part of the path to get there. This is what a facilitator can do and has been one of the goals of the book throughout.

There are people with good, mediocre, and bad managerial skills. A good manager is well respected and appreciated by all. A mediocre manager recognizes the need to improve the work environment but struggles and is clueless about where to begin, so it affects the performance of the whole team. A struggling manager is either someone who doesn't listen, thereby becoming the subject of everyone's fear and frustration, or someone unable to manage time and employees. It is for you to decide which legacy you want to be known for in your career. With the statistics and information shared in this book, we hope you can make the right decision and improve, no matter how good of a manager you are. If you do, be sure to follow the points and ideas shared. Make use of the tips that have been presented throughout this book so that you can become a great facilitator leader.

Remember, we want you to go home from work happy because your team is productive and engaged.

Chapter 8: Win the Team Game

Successful leaders and managers: This is a phrase used to describe effective, hardworking leaders who manage to do what mediocre ones don't – become successful!

Synonym for this includes *you* because you now have all the tools that will make it possible for you to be an accomplished, successful leader.

The simple concept that enables you to perform better and achieve more is teamwork. The workforce that you have in front of you is what will always be your strongest asset. This is a secret of corporate success very few managers realize, but those who do, benefit immensely from it. Most C-suite executives recognize the problem but aren't sure where to start, so a lot of hhcc4 is spent on multiple training theories, books, and programs.

No matter how qualified the people at work are, they will never be able to achieve goals and targets unless they are motivated and driven properly. The workforce will perform well in relaxed, friendly environments. Therefore, it is the role of the manager to encourage a friendly workplace and motivate the employees. To put it sophisticatedly, I would use the words of Brian Tracy, who once said, *"The best leaders have a high consideration factor and really care about their people."*

Throughout this book, we have revealed how to become not only a facilitative leader but also a balanced individual who engages their team through various teambuilding activities. We have disclosed how the rise of technology and e-communication has significantly impacted friendships at work. The statistics show how it has affected work performance and productivity. We have divulged most of what we teach in our workshops so that you can give your business a much-needed boost and create an engaging work environment for all.

This book has hopefully been quite the journey for you all. As much as we hope it taught you lessons in improving things at work, we also understand it can be quite a lot to take in. In order to win the Team Game, let's quickly review all that we discussed over the course of this book.

We shall begin by going back to the basics first — fun at work. For most managers, this is what challenges are made of. This is probably one of the common misconceptions where fun at work is associated with parties and celebrations, which is seen as equivalent to zero productivity. However, that is not the case. As explained, the idea of fun is an engaging and friendly environment where every employee feels valued and connected. In such environments, a manager or supervisor isn't the only person motivating employees to perform better. It is their co-workers who push them to perform better too. When one feels like they are a valued member of the team, they work hard to prove the truth behind that sentiment.

Meetings are a significant yet dreaded part of the work routine for most people. This is why fun at work starts at a meeting level. There are certain processes designed to engage people so that they look forward to showing up at meetings. We have experienced good and not-so-good meetings throughout our career with the outcome of engaged and not engaged. In our experience, we have heard from so many people who are uninterested in the meetings. Why? They feel undervalued for their time spent and that their feedback is not respected during the meetings.

The root cause of all this is disengagement and a frustrating work environment, to which people contribute as individuals also. We have seen firsthand how much things improve at work once the concept of fun is introduced in workplaces. Unfriendly work environments result in petty drama or conversation, usual misunderstanding, demotivated and unproductive workers, and losses. Fun is beneficial for employers and managers as it boosts creativity levels and healthy discussions. It extracts valuable feedback from employees on strategies that they have implemented. It dramatically increases productivity while decreasing employee absenteeism and turnover rate.

When workers enjoy their job and feel engaged, the environment automatically becomes friendly and healthy for everyone. Employees worldwide look forward to a happy work environment, so if yours falls under that category, it makes employees loyal to your company and brand. Once engaged, employees put in their efforts to work harder and perform better. They look forward to work and even meetings. Mondays become something that employees look forward to in healthy work environments.

Since 2000, we have seen that the concept of fun has slowly faded from work cultures. It has become something foreign to most managers and supervisors, which is why most businesses fail to reach their targets no matter how well they started off. For this reason, the concept of fun and engagement needs to be introduced to a company gradually.

Over the years, we have tried and tested several methods of team building. We have revealed our two most used and most favorite procedures: Team Talk and Team Workouts. They are the most helpful because they bring in positive results easily and quickly. These two work together to create an engaging and fun environment at work, making meetings and work hours enjoyable, productive, and something to look forward to. It is because Together Everyone Achieves More when engaged in a process.

Team Talk is an activity that helps all employees feel equal and valued. There is a table host who serves as a neutral person and engages all participants, i.e. the employees. Everyone is gathered at a table and given a problem that they have to solve or something they need to give their feedback on. The way the table host acts is very important as that makes the participants feel equal, valued, and engaged. This is the most effective and efficient way to bring team members together because the method encourages healthy communication and positive engagement.

Team Workouts are verbal, problem-solving, and guided exercises that help keep the team stay fit. These exercises are timed and require quick solutions and feedback from the team. The entire workforce is brought together and forced to solve problems within a defined time frame. This ensures that everyone acts naturally, impulsively, and without giving thought to their initial reservation or dislike against other group members. The way it works is for workers to come together and see each other in a different light, eventually forming lasting friendships.

Emotional and physical exhaustion are two very real issues that plague the life balance of many employees. They result in fatigue and a lack of creative ideas, among other serious work-related issues that can be damaging for both the company and the employee. This is why we urge both clients and readers to spend some team time engaging in meaningful activities that also serve as breaks. These breaks aren't pizza parties or ping pong games but meaningful activities that allow workers to Park and Recreate. We have reviewed what types of activities are beneficial, but our favorite is definitely volunteering and giving back to the community. VolunTEAMism helps team building in a way that you feel empowered and useful to those around you. It is very satisfying and rewarding and serves as the most satisfying *break*.

Our work life and personal life are very different, but they are interrelated. A person who overworks spends more time at work and, therefore, is unable to give time to their personal life. This can have many damaging consequences in the long run. People who underwork aren't very productive because they are unable to give time to their profession, resulting in almost immediate consequences. Both approaches are wrong. This is why as fun coaches, we encourage employees to maintain a balance through a dedicated work ethic and time commitment to healthy interests. Most importantly, we teach supervisors the importance and art of striking a work-life leisure balance. These activities help bring balance to you and your employees' lives. The self-time test will help you calculate and determine whether or not you have balanced your time in all areas of life.

We have always advocated for fun at work through better communication and cooperation or positive human interaction. We realized soon after working in this industry and promoting this approach that fun both away from work and at work is equally important. For this reason, we introduced the concept of fun away from work, its importance, and how it can be incorporated into team members. People who are happy away from work are the ones who show up at work with a better attitude toward people and team.

Here is a little exercise for all our readers that can help with this balance. You have been working so hard and feeling so drained that you need a break. Put on your oxygen mask first. Take the first 30 days to work on you away from work to focus on your work-life leisure balance schedule. Once you are done with this journey, you will see for yourself that when you return to work emotionally, you will be happier, rejuvenated, and more productive and creative. Don't just stop at the one-month break. Keep giving yourself scheduled weekly fun things to do. Give time to yourself and your loved ones, whether friends or family. You will notice the changes yourself soon enough.

To be a true leader, you must inspire your team, or your goals and vision will eventually expire. An example of true leadership isn't to create devoted followers or a fan-base but rather to create more leaders who inspire others. This is what we wish to teach all those who hope to become facilitators. Bring out the leader within you by inspiring those around you to become leaders too. The above three values, Team Talk, Team Workouts, and Work-life leisure balance, are required for fun at work.

Friendships, Unity, and Needs should be met for you to become a true source of inspiration and motivation for others. This is solely because these are team-building activities. You cannot become a facilitator unless you work with a team and build it up from mismatched individuals put together to a proper, unified, and engaged team. The art of facilitation starts with a small team and goes on to work its magic on bigger ones from that point onward.

Facilitating can be outsourced, but not only is it costly but also a challenge for time and perceived participant value. It is most effective if you do it yourself with your team because employees are likely to see the facilitator as an outsider. If you work on building your team up, you will earn the respect of all team members and they will view you as their true leader. We have discussed facilitative leadership and the methods that you can use to implement it. A true facilitator will use Team Talk to engage in meaningful conversations. There are several types of meetings. A good facilitative leader or manager will know the strategy and method to engage participants effectively to achieve desired results.

Good facilitative managers always work first on their problem-solving skills. Then they do workouts to sharpen the problem-solving skills of their team members. There are a lot of activities discussed that you can use, but always remember the real key lies in planning time where input from all team members is received prior to the planned activity (such as meetings). Implement and normalize conversations with your staff, such as "What worked?" "What didn't go so well?" or "What could we have done better?" to obtain continuous feedback. It serves as a learning tool and helps all managers to improve themselves, their ideas, their team, and their work. A true leader is one who learns from their mistakes and fixes them. The key isn't just the performance part of the activity, but it is also extremely important in how the people connect and work together. It is how they communicate in the process of it all.

Always focus on yourself first and then your team, although both have equal value. Watch how things work. Listen to the feedback. See for yourself what works for your business goals and objectives and also for your team, leadership skills, and style. Always learn from what is around you and then improve. Only then can you become the exemplary leader you desire for yourself. With that, we conclude Fun At Work for you and hope that it will serve you and your team well. It will help you to become a better and more engaging leader, bring your team closer, with all members feeling engaged and valued. Good luck with your future endeavors. Win the Team Game. Know that whatever happens, you will make it because you are a true, compassionate leader who is facilitative, adaptive, and always improving.

Like Your Work! Love Your Family! Enjoy Life! People who come to work happy usually leave happy! Remember, People First!

Bibliography

Choi Y, Jwon K, Kim W. (2020). Effects of Workplace Fun on Employee Behaviors: Focused on Generation Y in the Hospitality Industry. Retrieved fromhttps://scholarworks.umass.edu/cgi/viewcontent.cgi?article=1096&context=gradconf hospitality

McLeod S. (2020). Maslow's Hierarchy of Needs. Simply Psychology. Retrieved from https://www.simplypsychology.org/maslow.html

Tolman Walker. (2020). Why Employee Engagement Has a Direct Impact on Your Business Bottom Line. Retrieved from http://tolmanandwiker.com/employee-engagement-direct-impact-business-bottom-line/

(2020). Lack of engagement in the workplace. Retrieved from https://appliedpsychologydegree.usc.edu/blog/lack-of-engagement-in-the-workplace/

The State of Meeting Reports 2019. Doodle. Retrieved from https://meeting-report.com/

(2020). 12 different types of leadership styles. Wise Toast. Retrieved from https://wisetoast.com/types-of-leadership-styles/

Made in the USA
Middletown, DE
13 February 2022

60815353R00061